AMERICAN RESOLVE
AND THE ART OF WAR

A Study and Application of Military Tactics

John Proctor

authorHOUSE®

AuthorHouse™
1663 Liberty Drive
Bloomington, IN 47403
www.authorhouse.com
Phone: 1-800-839-8640

Published by AuthorHouse 9/26/2012

ISBN: 978-1-4772-5758-6 (sc)
ISBN: 978-1-4772-5757-9 (hc)
ISBN: 978-1-4772-5759-3 (e)

Library of Congress Control Number: 2012914252

TABLE OF CONTENTS

PREFACE

THE SPANISH-AMERICAN PHILOSOPHER, George Santayana, wrote, "Those who do not remember the past are condemned to relive it." Many times, however, world leaders are, powerless to control events. Great issues are like snowballs gathering mass and momentum as they roll down a hill. Statesmen cannot or will not believe what is happening until it is too late. Then, as Winston Churchill observed, "The terrible Ifs accumulate."

French King Louis XIV, who reigned between 1643 and 1715, recognized the limitations of statesmen and ordered an inscription engraved on the tubes of his cannon, *Ultima Ratio Regis* or The Last Argument of Kings. War was the only way kings and heads of state could dispose of differences. Lesser men relied upon the courts to reconcile their differences. Kings were not bound by a court and, therefore, their differences were decided by the judgment of battle.

Carl von Clausewitz supports the French king by his dictum, "War is a continuation of policy by other means." The Communist dictator, Mao Tse-tung, was more direct, "Political power grows from a barrel of a gun."

No one wants war. At least, no sane person wants war. At times, nevertheless, war is seemingly inevitable. In 1860, the so-called Cotton States of the Southern United States did not want a war. They only wanted to maintain their agricultural economy that was based primarily on the production of cotton and tobacco. The Northern leaders, principally Abraham Lincoln, wanted to preserve the union and abolish slavery. The election of Lincoln as president was then a signal to the South that their economy would be destroyed. Slavery was an endemic part of the Southern economy. If their economy were destroyed, Southern culture and social order would also be destroyed. The South then wanted to form a separate nation, but President Lincoln resolved to preserve the union. The differences between the North and the South could not be reconciled by negotiation. Thus, the judgment of battle was the only alternative.

In 1939, the Soviet Union demanded Finland yield 1,000 square miles of territory, mostly in the Leningrad area, in return for 2,000 square miles in the Karelia that was almost a wasteland. Finland rejected the Soviet demand. The Soviet foreign minister then said, "It will now be for the soldiers to negotiate."{P-1}

Prior to the outbreak of World War II, Hitler, the dictator of Germany, marched his troops into the Rhineland in violation of the Versailles Treaty. He then marched into Austria without firing a shot. Czechoslovakia was next. Several of Europe's great powers sought to negotiate with Hitler in an effort to avert war. Britain, France, and Italy met with Hitler and decided the best course was to cede the Sudetenland, a mountainous region in Western Czechoslovakia populated by German-speaking people, to Germany.

At the same time, Hitler precipitated another crisis by demanding from Poland the city of Danzig and the Polish Corridor, a strip of land separating the province of East Prussia from the main part of Germany and a part of Germany until 1919. Poland refused to yield the territory, and in September 1939, Germany invaded Poland and World War II began. War was the only alternative.

At the end of World War II, the United States had hoped for a „one world" with faith in the newly created United Nations to act as the world's policeman, judge, and welfare agency. The United States wanted to promote political, social, and ideological changes that would lead to world stability. Regrettably, people, nations, and governments are never quite satisfied. Perhaps it is a basic human failing. Man, after all, was originally in the Garden of Eden but was not satisfied.

There have been many theories and reasons for wars. Some suggest war is caused by the competition over resources, the materialist view. War is the result of historical and cultural differences, the historical view. War arises from individuals struggling for reproductive success, the socio-biological view. Others attempt to describe the nature and purpose of war through two general theories. War is a rational undertaking initiated to achieve certain desired results and can be controlled by the application of reason. The second theory is that war is an act of blind passion, controlled by demonic powers of darkness and is incapable of serving any rational or useful purpose.

Mankind has always had a dream of creating an eternally peaceful world. In recent history, the world held The Hague Peace Conference of 1899 and 1907, the London Naval Conference of 1908, and the Washington Conference of 1921. In January 1918, President Wilson gave hope to a war weary world with his Fourteen Points Speech that would establish a perpetual peace for the world. In more recent times, the United States and the Soviet Union and subsequently Russia have engaged in Strategic Arms Limitation Talks, Strategic Arms Reduction talks, and Mutual and Balanced Force Reductions. All of these talks and conferences are worthwhile, but they have not averted war.

In 1898, a Warsaw economist and Polish railway magnate, Jean De Bloch, wrote a six-volume book, *The Future of War in its Technical, Economic and Political Relations: Is War Now Impossible?* The original work was published in Polish, Russian, French, and German. After studying the writings of many military authorities, Bloch concluded that the increased power of modern firearms made war impossible except at the price of suicide. The book influenced Czar Nikolas II in 1898 to call for an arms limitation among the world powers that ultimately led to the Hague Conference of 1899.

Since the publication of this book, the world was involved in two world wars and hundreds of lesser wars. After the end of World War II, fifteen million Americans have served in what may be called low intensity conflicts, and 115,000 Americans have died in them.

In 1790, President George Washington, in a speech before both houses of Congress advised, "To be prepared for war is one of the most effectual means of preserving peace." The Romans supported this view: *si vis pacem, para bellum* (if you want peace, prepare for war.) (P-2) The British military historians, Liddel Hart, though, concluded that after his studies of war, a more accurate maxim would be, "If you wish for peace, understand war."

CHAPTER 1

A GLEAM OF STEEL

EVENTS THAT LEAD to the Second World War included the Sudetenland crisis. The Sudetenland was a mountainous region in Western Czechoslovakia that was inhabited by 3.5 million German-speaking people. Before World War I, the region was part of Austria and on the border with Germany. The region was mishandled by the treaties ending World War I.

Before the end of World War I, Czechoslovakia including the Sudetenland was a part of the Austrian Empire. Since Austria was allied with Germany in the war, Austria was treated as harshly as Germany in the Treaty of Versailles. Before the end of the First World War the Austrian Empire included not only Austria but also Hungary, Czechoslovakia, parts of Poland, Romania, Italy and Yugoslavia. The prewar area of the empire encompassed 261,029 square miles and included 51 million people. After the treaty, Austria had only six million people that encompassed 32,369 square miles. {1-1} This was done under the guise of self-determination.

Self-determination had merit, but the war's losers should have had a voice in the consequences. The Sudeten Germans were part of German-speaking Austria. By treaty, the Sudeten Germans suddenly became part of another country that was dominated by another people speaking another language... A cursory review of a map would readily indicate that the Sudetenland should have been made part of Germany. This would follow geographic logic and satisfy self-determination. Germany, however, lost the war and could not be granted additional territory.

Winston Churchill wrote, "The second cardinal tragedy was the complete breakup of the Austro-Hungarian Empire by the Treaties of St. Germain and Trianon. For centuries this surviving embodiment of

1

the Holy Roman Empire had afforded a common life, with advantages in trade and security, to a large number of peoples, none of whom in our own time had the strength of vitality to stand by themselves in the face of pressure from a revivified Germany or Russia. All these races wished to break away from the federal or imperial structure, and to encourage their desires was deemed a liberal policy." {1-2)

Nevertheless, the treaties were accomplished and the next generation had to suffer the consequences. One of the consequences was Adolph Hitler. It cannot be said that the Treaty of Versailles resulted in the direct rise of Adolph Hitler. It can be said, though, that the treaty made it easy for a person like Hitler to succeed.

The Germans believed that they would discuss a peace treaty ending World War I under the "Pact of November 5, 1918." that pledged they would negotiate within the framework of President Wilson's Fourteen Points. Wilson's Fourteen Points amounted to the internationalization of the American Declaration of Independence, The Constitution and the Monroe Doctrine. This was very idealistic, but if accepted, it would have led to conciliation and peace.

The tiger of France, Georges Clemenceau who represented France, said, "God gave us the Ten Commandments, and we broke them. Wilson gave us the Fourteen Points, and we will see." The British representative, Lloyd George, said of the treaty negotiations, "It was like sitting between Napoleon Bonaparte and Jesus Christ." Clemenceau was determined to punish Germany. Wilson, above all else, wanted a League of Nations. Therefore, a compromise resulted. Germany was to be punished but Wilson got his League of Nations.

Germany was particularly incensed by the so-called "War Guilt Clause." {1-3} Article 231 of the Treaty of Versailles reads:

> "The Allied and Associated Governments affirm and Germany accepts the responsibility of Germany and her allies for causing all the loss and damage to which the Allied and Associated Governments and their nationalities have been subjected as a consequence of the war imposed upon them by the aggression of Germany and her allies."

In truth, Europe in 1914 was two armed camps: The Triple Alliance and the Triple Entente. All that was needed was a spark to set Europe in flames. Germany, Austria and Italy formed the Triple Alliance, while Britain, France and Russia formed the Triple Entente.

France and Russia formed a bond that was clearly intended to provoke a European war. The Franco-Russian Alliance was probably initiated about 1892. {1-4} Raymond Poincare, the French Premier and Foreign Minister, who was born in Lorrain and witnessed French humiliation at the hands of the Germans when it was defeated in the Franco-Prussian War of 1871, wanted vengeance on Germany. Baron Izvolski, a Russian diplomat, plotted with Poinare to start a European War; so that Russia could obtain Constantinople and the Turkish Straits between the Black Sea and the Mediterranean Sea. The Russians coveted the Turkish Straits since the reign of Catherine the Great. (1762-1796){1-5}

Russia had contemplated a war without allies against Turkey. {1-6} In this scenario, Russia realized that the German Navy may intercede in Turkey's behave. Thus, it would be expedient to await a general European War, whereby Russia could obtain allies such as the British and French fleets that could neutralize the German naval threat.

Russia did not have long to wait for a European crisis to develop and lead to a general European war. For some time, Serbia, a nation in the South Balkans, was going through a wave of nationalism. These feelings were intensified when Austria in 1908 annexed two-neighboring countries: Bosnia and Herzegovina. These states were inhabited by Slavs like Serbia. The Serbs felt that the annexation was aggressive and utterly unjustified. {1-7}

Austria intended to institute liberal reforms in its newly acquired states. Archduke Franz Ferdinand, the heir apparent to the Austrian throne, planned a triune monarchy to give more liberties to Austrian Slavs. Germans, Hungarians and Slavs would be equal in the empire. Nationalists in Serbia realized that the archduke must be assassinated before the reforms could be instituted. More liberties for Austria's newly acquired Slavic states would cement Bosnia's and Herzegovina's desire to be attached to Austria. This would destroy any plans for a Greater Serbia. {1-8}.

Thereupon, Serbia enlisted some Bosnian adventurers for assassination training in Belgrade, Serbia. The Serbian military trained the adventurers in the use of firearms and bomb throwing. {1-9} Afterwards, they were sent to Sarajevo, Bosnia and waited for the arrival of the archduke Russia was also culpable in the assassination plot, as it supplied munitions to the plotters in Serbia. {1-10}

On June 28, 1914, the assassination plot was successfully carried-out. Austria immediately accused Serbia of complicity in the assassination. The only evidence Austria had of Serbia's culpability in the plot was newspaper articles in the Serbian press and the general attitude of the Serbian government {1-11} Diplomats attempted to resolve the dispute but were unsuccessful. Austria then declared war on Serbia July 28, 1914. {1-12}

Although Russia held no alliances with Serbia, it felt compelled to support Serbia. {1-13} Russia and Serbia were both ethnic Slavs and both followed the same orthodox religion. Russia also wanted a general European war without the onus of starting the war. When officials in the Russian government were informed of the Austrian ultimatum to Serbia, the Russian foreign minister, Sazonov, exclaimed, "This is the European war!"{1-14}

At 6:00 p.m. on July 30, 1914, the final general mobilization order was sent out by the Russian government. The Russians knew that this order actually and technically meant the beginning of a European war. General Dobrorolski, chief of the mobilization division of the Russian army wrote, "This (the mobilization order) once fixed there is no way backwards. This step settles automatically the beginning of war. This affair now began irretrievably. The order was already well known in all the larger cities of our huge country. No change was possible. The prologue of the great historic drama had begun."{1-15} A few days later, other European nations followed Russia to war. At 4:00 p.m. August 1, 1914, France gave the mobilization order. Germany followed 30 minutes later {1-16} Britain waited until August 4, 1914 to declare war. {1-17}

None of the European governments had any foreknowledge of the horrific war that would be fought. When Kaiser Wilhelm addressed his troops departing to the front, he said, "You will be home before the leaves have fallen from the trees."{1-18} "The French counted mainly on the active army of about one million men to strike the blows in the short, victorious campaign they expected."{1-19}

France developed Plan XVII, which emphasized elan, the offensive spirit. General Ferdinand Foch, commandant of the French Ecole Superieure de la Guerre, was convinced that the indomitable will to win was the major ingredient to victory. Other French officers, such as Colonel Louzeau de Grandmaison, enhanced this view and presumed the French military doctrine was: to attack at all costs, at all times, and under any circumstance, *l'offensive a' outrance*. {1-21} Defensive thought was despised. The entrenching spade was abandoned. "To dig one's self in diminishes the intensity of one's fire and depresses the offensive spirit." {1-22} The French plan was to launch an offense assault through Alsace-Lorain and then head straight for Berlin.

Germany prepared the Schlieffen Plan that would deploy the German Army to advance west through the Belgian Plain and follow along the English Channel to a point west of Paris and then wheel about and attack the rear of the French Army and destroy it. The German General Staff had anticipated that the French Army would attack through Alsace-Lorain. Therefore, Germany would deploy a relatively small defensive force in Alsace-Lorain to oppose the French axis of attack. Consequently, the main German force closing from the west would become the hammer and the German defense force near Alsace-Lorain would become the anvil.

These plans rapidly fell apart. Most war plans never survive the first battle. The early battles conveyed to the European leaders the harbinger of the European war that lay ahead. Ypres was one of the first battles. The battle takes its name from a small town in Belgium that lies near the North Sea. The battle began on October 20, 1914, {1-23} and subsided on November 11, 1914 at a cost of 130,000 German casualties, 58,000 British casualties and about 250,000 French casualties. {1-24} When Lord Kitchener, the British Secretary of State for War, was made aware of the casualty figures he immediately exclaimed, "This isn't war!"

The Ypres Battle foretold a war of attrition. A war of attrition is the worst kind of war, as it emphasizes the killing of enemy troops. Its objective is to wear-down the enemy and force him to meet your will. Military tactics are minimized, as only head long frontal attacks are ordered. Mounting casualties are ignored.

A war of attrition, if it goes on for more than a year, becomes an infectious disease. Troops in each opposing army begin to believe that the enemy troops are less than human. They will shoot prisoners; bayonet the wounded and mutilate the bodies of fallen enemy soldiers. Mounting casualty figures sent to kinsmen back home will infect the civilian population. They in turn will demand that their government take more brutal action against the enemy. When it's time to sign a peace treaty, justice will not prevail. The winning side possesses the judge, jury and prosecutor. The peace treaty at Versailles, as understood by the Germans, was not negotiated. It was imposed and became known as the *diktat of Versailles{I-25}*. It paved the way for another horrific war. . . .

The Ypres battle had arisen too soon. The soldiers on both sides were ill-prepared for the battle. Their training and tactics were obsolete in the face of advanced technology such as machine guns, barbed wire and heavy artillery. American historian, Richard M. Watt, wrote of the battle, "The generals are to be blamed not so much because they failed to open up the trench war as because they *went on trying to do it*, wasting thousands of lives with each attempt, long after it should have been apparent that they could not succeed with the old methods."{1-26} Albert Einstein defined insanity, "doing the same thing over and over again and expecting different results."{1-27} German general Max Hoffman's term for the stubborn British generals: "the donkeys." Though, the British generals concluded after Ypres, "We must dig deeper!"{1-28}.

Digging deeper was the order of the day. Both armies dug deep pits to protect their troops from heavy artillery bombardments. Consequently, a continuous, 400 mile trench line was dug from the North Sea to the Swiss frontier. Seven German armies then faced eight French armies plus the British Expeditionary Force and the Belgian Army. From December 1914 until November 1918, a stalemate existed along the 400-mile front. Each side attacked the other's trenches but made little progress other than inflicting more casualties. After three years, the trench line did not vary more than 10 miles. {1-29}.

The main hypothesis of the Schlieffen Plan was to prevent Germany from fighting a war on two fronts. Germany was aware of the Franco-Russian alliance. In the event of a war with both Russia and France, the bulk of the German Army would crush France in the West during the first weeks of the war and then turn about and assault the slower mobilizing Russian Army in the East. After the first weeks, however, France was not crushed, and two Russian armies were converging on the German province of East Prussia. Germany then found itself fighting a war it wanted to avoid: a war on two fronts. Germany though, had an advantage: it geographically separated its two adversaries; so that they could not directly support one another. Also, Germany had an excellent rail system that could quickly shift troops from one front to the other

By December 1914, Germany held most of Belgium and a large portion of Northern France. Germany then opted for defense in the West, as much of its army had to be deployed to the East. In 1915, Germany was outnumbered by a ratio of three to one in the West. {1-30} Thus, Germany adopted an elastic defense system in the West: The initial, or front line trench had two or more widely separated defense trenches dug-in behind it. When assaulting troops broke through the initial trench, they were decimated by troops in the secondary defense trenches. {1-31} In WWII, this defense system was known as a *pak-front*. {1-32}

The Battle of Ypres fought in October-November, 1914, became known as First Ypres. Two more battles were fought at Ypres. Second Ypres was between April 22 and May 25, 1915, at a cost of 60,000 British casualties and 10,000 French casualties. Third Ypres was fought from July 31 to November 10, 1917 at a cost of some 300,000 British casualties and 8,528 French casualties.

Other significant battles fought along the 400-mile Western Front were: Verdun in 1916, which cost the French some 542,000 casualties; Somme in 1916, which cost the British 420,000 casualties and France 195,000 casualties, Aisne in 1917 which cast the French 120,000 casualties, and the Cambrai in 1917, which cost the British 45,000 casualties.

The total World War I casualties for three nations were as follows: France, 5,623,800; British Empire, 2,998,583; Germany: 6,055,689 {1-33} These casualty figures represent losses as a percent of the total forces mustered as follows: France 67 percent; British Empire 34 percent, and Germany 55 percent. None of these nations wished for another war. :

France, after the war, became passivist and defensive. Its dominate emphasis was: *Securite*. {1-34} The 1914 spirit of elan was totally dismissed. Between 1929 and 1934, France constructed the Maginot Line, a series of concrete and steel fortifications placed opposite the German frontier. {1-35} Additionally, between 1920 and 1926, it made military alliances with Belgium, Poland and the so-called "Little Entente" composed of Czechoslovakia, Rumania, and Yugoslavia, {1-36} This was known as the "Iron Ring" around Germany, which caused consternation within Germany.

Britain, too, lost interest in European affairs.

> "Well over one million were unemployed, economic recovery was slow in coming. What, these people asked, what had been gained in winning World War I? What would be gained by winning--or losing--another war against the dictators? Students of the Oxford Union, which had provided generations of British leaders, now voted for a resolution: That this house refuses to fight for King and Country."{1-37}

The Versailles Treaty burdened Germany with reparations in the amount of $56 billion. The treaty also limited Germany to a 100,000 man army. The artillery guns were limited in size to 75 millimeters. The German Army could have no tanks or military aircraft. The General Staff was abolished. Moreover, the frontiers were adjusted so as to permit a quick suppression of any German military resistance. {1-38} A Polish Army could occupy Berlin after a two-day march. {1-39}

In 1923, Belgium and France declared that Germany was in default in reparation payments. Thus on January 11, 1923, they sent-in troops to occupy the German industrial district, the Ruhr Valley. {1-40}. The German workers in the district refused to work under the foreign occupation, which caused the German currency to devalue. In 1921, under the Versailles reparations policy, the German Mark depreciated to one percent of its prewar value. In October 1923, one American dollar was equivalent to 4.2 trillion marks. {1-41}

Germany, at the time, was in economic chaos, which was aggravated by French fear of a German war of revenge, and also the desire to punish Germany. The German people began to mistrust the victors in the World War. The Weimar Republic, which was to bring democracy to Germany, became an object of derision, as it was imposed by the Versailles Treaty.

The punitive tenets of the Versailles Treaty and its unrealistic demands were the reaction to the devastating long war of attrition. During the war, the military leaders in both armies had believed that the only way to break the stalemate in France was to force a breakthrough by sheer weight of numbers. A basic problem in the West was the front was too small for the vast number of troops engaged. The opposing armies could not maneuver. A war of attrition was the only alternative.

The preferred battle plan is to fight a war of maneuver. A war of maneuver requires not only the military commander but also his subordinates to be highly skilled in military tactics and operations. The main objective in a war of maneuver is not to slaughter enemy troops but to deploy forces in such a manner that the enemy realizes that he must either retreat or surrender.

World War I began as a war of maneuver, but after a few weeks, it digressed into a war of attrition. The Schlieffen Plan was not fully implemented and, consequently, the German Army's invasion was halted at the Marne River. The French Plan XVII was not realistic in the face of heavy artillery, barbed wire, and machine guns. . . . .

The American Civil War was a war of attrition and a war of maneuver. Generally, the Northern Army fought mostly a war of attrition and the Southern Army mostly fought a war of maneuver. The South was at a decided disadvantage. Therefore, a war of maneuver was its only option.

The North should have easily won the war within six months. During the entire war, the North raised military forces of nearly three million men. The South could rise only three quarters of a million men. {1-42} The North held 23 states with a population of about 23 million. The South held 11 states with a white population of five million people. {1-43} The Southern economy was based upon agriculture; the North upon manufacturing.

Anticipating a short conflict, President Lincoln called for 75,000 volunteers to serve three months. Two weeks later, he requested another 42,000 men to serve three years or until the war was over. {1-44} President Lincoln was not aware of the considerable military skills possessed by two Southern generals, Robert E. Lee and "Stonewall" Jackson. The war was to go on for four years.

The North with its superior numbers simply wore down the South in a war of attrition. Many Northern generals tried to win victories while limiting casualties but were unsuccessful. Therefore, Lincoln turned to General Grant to win the war through attrition. Northern newspapers referred to the Union Commander as, "Grant the butcher"{1-45}.

In the Vietnam War, the US fought a war of attrition. The Vietnam War began long before the US involvement. The war began in the 1920s as an anti colonial movement. After World War II, the Potsdam agreement provided that Vietnam be liberated by the Chinese in the North and the British in the South. Britain did not have the troops available; so France undertook this responsibility. In 1954, France lost a major battle to the North Vietnamese Army. In July 1954 the Geneva Accords were signed which split Vietnam along the 17th Parallel. North Vietnam was Communist and South Vietnam was supposedly Democratic. The US elected to support the South as a bastion against the Communist. In 1957, the Communists made guerilla attacks on the South Vietnamese government

The US commander of Military Assistance Command Vietnam, Army General William C. Westmoreland, devised the military plan of attrition. He believed that "search and destroy" operations could win the war by inflicting more casualties than the enemy could endure. {1-

46) Westmoreland believed that Vietnam was "an enemy with limited manpower."{1-47} Although, in 1961, General Douglas MacArthur had cautioned President Kennedy of the dangers in committing an American force to the Asian mainland. {1-48}

In 1967, President Lyndon Johnson announced that the search and destroy tactics plus heavy bombing raids against North Vietnam had severely curtailed the infiltration along the Ho Chi Minh Trail. {1-49} "Light at the end of the tunnel"{1-50} was proclaimed by US forces. The war appeared to be winding down.

Then, as a complete surprise, The North Vietnamese Army launched the Tet Offensive in January 1968. Tet is the Vietnamese New Year, and the North Vietnamese believed that the South Vietnamese would be in a relaxed state while observing the event. The offensive attacked the South Vietnamese capital, Saigon, and other provincial capitals. Militarily, the Tet Offensive was a complete failure, as the South Vietnamese Army plus American troops quickly put down the attack.

Politically, the offensive was absolutely successful. The idea of enemy troops shooting-up the South's capital gave a clear indication that the war was not going well. Finally in January 1973, the Paris Peace Accords were signed. The agreement allowed the withdrawal of American troops and a cease fire.

The Vietnam War and World War I ended with peace agreements in Paris. Shortly after the Vietnam War ended, all of Vietnam became communist. The agreement to end World War I did not fare much better. Without trying to resolve all the critical issues, it would seem that the treaty to end World War I created an environment for World War II.

Adolf Hitler became chancellor of Germany in 1933. By coincidence, Franklin Roosevelt became president of the US in 1933. Both men had the tremendous task of overcoming severe economic depressions. The depression in the US was terrible. The depression in Germany was much worse. The most tragic part of the depression was the high rates of unemployed people. A man identifies himself by the job he holds. If a man has no job, he is nothing. His self-esteem goes to zero. Very few Americans living today can recall life in the US during the depression. A film depicting the depression era, *The Grapes of Wrath*, is a good reminder of this era.

Adolf Hitler and Franklin Roosevelt put their countrymen back to work. Consequently, each leader became extremely popular in their respective countries. Popular understated the feeling of the populous. Their true feeling had to be revered. Hitler and Roosevelt could do no wrong in the eyes of the common people.

To bring the country out of the depression, Roosevelt introduced many new concepts. His overall position was the "New Deal." {1-51} He tried to institute the National Recovery Act {1-52}, but this was ruled unconstitutional by the Supreme Court. However, the Works Progress Administration and the Civilian Conservation Corps were acceptable by the Supreme Court. {1-53}

Hitler, by contrast, had no Supreme Court to keep his power in check. Also, there was not a democratic tradition in Germany as there was in the US. In Germany: there was only one body that had the tradition and prestige to override a government decision, the General Staff. The Versailles Treaty prevented Germany from having a General Staff. Thus, senior German officers assumed this responsibility. The German officers were not concerned with the legality or the justice of a decision. Their main concern was the welfare of Germany. They did not want Germany to enter a ruinous war or enter a war when the odds were very much against Germany.

Hitler's overall doctrine was the "New Order." The Reichstag, Germany's parliament, passed the "Enabling Act," which gave Hitler absolute power for four years. The parliament also decreed that only one political party, the National Socialist, was to function in Germany. {1-54}

On December 11, 1932, the Disarmaments Conference, under the auspices of the League of Nations, recognized equal rights for Germany in principle. {1-55} There were, however, certain conditions attached. There had to be a formula for a security guarantee. Germany and other disarmed nations could not re-arm too rapidly or too comprehensively. Hitler rejected the conditions imposed by the Disarmament Conference and dissolved the Reichstag. He then called for a new election on the issue of foreign policy. In the November 1933 election, the National Socialist won by an overwhelming majority. This showed the world that the German people were united behind Hitler on the disarmament question. Germany then withdrew from the League of Nations and the Disarmament Conference. Hitler then felt that he could openly risk rearmament of the German Army.

Hitler's next objective was incorporating Austria into Germany. The German Army was not up to the task. Thus, National Socialist within Austria had to accomplish this objective without open German assistance. On July 25, 1934, the Austrian Chancellor, Englebert Dolfus, was murdered within the Austrian Chancellery. It appeared that Hitler had won. However the new chancellor, Kurt Schuschnigg, was courageous and held Hitler at bay. Chancellor Schuschnigg was aided in this endeavor by the dictator of Italy, Benito Mussolini. This aid was in the form of three Italian army divisions dispatched to the Brenner Pass with the intent to intervene in Austria if it were to be incorporated into Germany. {1-56}

Hitler then realized that he had to have an army to accomplish his goals. Therefore, in violation of the Versailles Treaty, he proclaimed military conscription in Germany on March 16, 1935. World leaders became alarmed. But, however, Germany was cast in the background by the action of Mussolini. At a conference with other European powers on April 11-14, 1935, Mussolini mentioned his invasion plan of Ethiopia. Italy possessed a small colony, Eritrea, bordering Ethiopia, which would be used as a base to invade Ethiopia. France favored Mussolini's invasion plan as a way to secure Italy's support against Hitler. Britain, though, was totally against the invasion plan and the British public rose-up in protest. The French government leaders were forced to resign. Mussolini became incensed with statements made in public by British government leaders. As a result, Mussolini then became closer to Hitler. {1-57}

Hitler's next move was to militarize the Rhineland, which was a clear violation of Article 43 of the Versailles Treaty. During the night of March 7, 1936, 35,000 German troops crossed the boundary and entered all the main German towns. The German generals agreed with Hitler's move into the Rhineland with the condition that German troop commanders order a retreat automatically if they met any French military resistance. {1-58} The French Army at the time had 100 divisions. If these troops had been mobilized and sent to the Rhineland, the German troops would have retreated and probably cause the downfall of Hitler. {1-59}.

The climate of conviction in France at that time was insecurity. The French government was in transition, as the premier was in office only until the new election established a new premier. To mobilize the army may be construed as an act of war against Germany. France did not want to make a decision without the concurrence of Britain. {1-60} Britain, for its part, advised France to present the case before the League of Nations. Ultimately, nothing was done. Hitler had won.

At the time, France was the leader of the "Iron Ring," which was composed of Belgium, Poland, Czechoslovakia, Yugoslavia and Romania. French indecisiveness caused the lesser nation in the "Iron Ring" to doubt French conviction. Without committed French leadership, the smaller "Iron Ring" nations became uneasy.

Subsequently, the German Army became stronger both in numbers and in maturity plus quality of its formations. {1-61} The Rhineland became fortified with permanent and semipermanent fortifications and then named "The West Wall." Hitler was now ready to secure Austria.

The Austrian chancellor, Schuschnigg, remained defiant. He tried to hold a plebiscite on the question of union with Germany. {1-62} Events in Austria, including political intrigue, then moved very fast. Schuschnigg was forced to resign, and he was replaced by Arthur von Seyss-Inquart who promptly agreed to all of Hitler's demands. These events occurred on Mach 8, 1938. {1-63}.

Mussolini, who interceded in Austria's behalf in 1934, was ready to intercede again. At the time, Italy was negotiating a treaty with Britain. Mussolini made it clear to Britain that Italy could not resist the German occupation of Austria until the agreement with Britain was completed. The British cabinet could not come to a collective conclusion, as British public opinion was in favor of a union between Austria and Germany. Hitler won again.

Hitler's next objective was Czechoslovakia. Thereupon Hitler ordered the general staff to draft plans for the invasion of Czechoslovakia. The German generals balked at this decision. They were aware of British and French pacifism and weakness, but they could not believe that Hitler could succeed a fourth time. .Britain and France did nothing when Hitler ordered military conscription, occupied the Rhineland, and occupied Austria. Now, he wanted to attack Czechoslovakia.

Hitler, though, was convinced that Britain and France would not fight for Czechoslovakia. {1-64} Hitler was negotiating from strength. He held all the high cards. These cards were the World War I battles of the Somme, Verdun, Ypres and many others. Millions of young British and French men were slaughtered on the bloody battlefields of France. The British and French governments would do most anything to avoid another bloody confrontation with Germany.

Germany, too, suffered heavy casualties in World War I. Hitler, being a dictator, answered to no one except, perhaps, the German

General Staff. The general staff was aware of the military -strength of Germany versus Britain, France, Czechoslovakia and Russia. The Czech Army had constructed the Bohemian Fortress Line facing Germany in the east. To break the line would require 35 German divisions. In the west, France could muster 100 divisions, while Germany would have only five effective divisions and eight reserve divisions to face them. {1-65}

The chief of the German General Staff, General Ludwig von Beck sent a memorandum to Hitler outlining in detail the military facts as to the differences between Germany and its adversaries. At present, Germany was at a military disadvantage. {1-66} If Germany were forced into a war, it would surely be crushed. The resultant treaty would probably be more severe than the Versailles Treaty.

General Beck confronted Hitler personally and demanded that Hitler not engage Germany into further military adventures. Hitler advised Beck that the Army was an instrument of the State, and he was the head of State. Therefore, the Army owed Hitler unquestioning obedience to his will. With this, General Beck resigned his post. {1-67} Hitler then appointed General Franz Halder to replace him.

Hitler's invasion plan was subtle. He would use political intrigue that was always supported by the bloody battles of World War I. The World War I battles were not mentioned in the negotiations, but they were always present as an unseen back drop.

Hitler did not plan to occupy all of Czechoslovakia in a single stroke. He would first seek the Sudetenland, an area occupied by 3.5 million German speaking people. Hitler first demanded full autonomy for the Sudeten Germans. Britain and France wavered at this demand. Hitler then demanded full incorporation of the Sudetenland into Germany. {1-68}.

Before the Treaty of Versailles, the Sudetenland was part of Austria not only linguistically but also historically, culturally and ethnically. The people were part of Austria for hundreds of years and were part of the ethnic majority until the Treaty of Versailles. Their capital was Vienna. After Versailles, their capital was Prague. They became part of another country with a different language and culture. They were now a minority.

London and Paris were aware of the plight of the Sudeten Germans, which made negotiations with Hitler more difficult. The plight of Sudeten Germans had to be weighed against the aggressive behavior of Adolf

Hitler. Moreover, France had a treaty obligation with Czechoslovakia. In 1924, France and Czechoslovakia made a treaty binding the two countries together to come to the other's aide in the event of an attack from Germany. Subsequently, Czechoslovakia supported France in every international political endeavor {1-69}. . .

British and French negotiations with Hitler were troublesome, as Czechoslovakia's treaty with France was similar to the one made with the Soviet Union. If the Soviet Union went to war in defense of Czechoslovakia, Germany might lose the war, which could bring the Soviet Army into Europe and then all of Europe might be engulfed in Communism. In recent Czech elections, the Communist made successful inroads, which alarmed many Czechs. {1-70} Moreover, British and French generals concluded that their air defenses were lagging behind Germany's. {1176} They had a genuine fear that British and French cities could be destroyed by serial bombardment without recourse.

Unknown to the British and French governments, at this time, was a plot to depose Hitler by the German generals. The former chief of staff, General Beck, was well respected by other German generals and believed his military judgment was sound. General Halder, General Beck's successor, and six other top ranking German generals agreed with General Beck. {1-71} The generals concluded that Hitler was leading Germany to disaster. Therefore, they planned to arrest Hitler and his top associates and establish a military government. Afterwards, they would issue a proclamation to the German people that this action was necessary to prevent Hitler from leading Germany to ruin. {1-72}

This action could only come about with a strong resolve by Britain and France regarding the Sudetenland. If Britain and France failed in their resolve, the German generals could not act. Hitler was far too popular among the German people. If Britain and France had a weak resolve and Hitler got his way, the German generals would look very foolish in the eyes of the German people. The people would probably drag the generals through the streets and hang them to a lamp post.

To avert war, Britain and France sought to negotiate with Hitler. On September 15, 1938, British Chancellor of the Exchequer, Neville Chamberlain, met with Adolf Hitler at Berchtesgaden, Germany. Chamberlain sought regional autonomy for the Sudeten Germans. Hitler wanted annexation of the Sudeten Germans. {1-73} The meeting seemed to come to an impasse. Chamberlain did conclude: "In spite of the hardness and ruthlessness I thought I saw in his face, I got the impression that here was a man who could be relied upon when he had given his word." Hitler assured Chamberlain, "This is the last territorial claim I have to make in Europe." {1-74}

Chamberlain and Hitler decided to hold a second meeting. The meeting was held on September 22, 1938 at Godesberg, Germany. This time Hitler issued an ultimatum: On Saturday, October 1, the German Army would march into the territories concerned unless the Czechs acquiesced by 2:00 P.M. Wednesday, September 28.

London and Paris decided to reject the Godesberg terms. France, Britain and Czechoslovakia mobilized their armed forces. On June 12, 1938, the French government had declared, "France's engagements toward Czechoslovakia 'are sacred, and cannot be evaded.'"{1-75} Chamberlain, in desperation to avert war, drafted a personal message to Hitler. His letter proposed that another meeting be held in Germany with representatives from Britain, France Italy, Czechoslovakia and Germany. Chamberlain telegraphed Mussolini of this proposal. {1-76}

Hitler accepted the proposed meeting and delayed his ultimatum to mobilize for 24 hours. Hitler invited Chamberlain, the French Premier Edouard Daladier, and Mussolini to meet with him in Munich, Germany. Czechoslovakia and the Soviet Union were not invited. {1-77} The meeting began at noon and did not end until 2:00 a.m. the next morning on September 30. "The Big Four" accepted the Godesberg ultimatum. The Sudetenland was to be evacuated in five stages beginning October 1 and completed in 10 days.

The Czechs were not invited to the conference but were invited to sign the memorandum agreement made by "The Big Four." The Czechs could militarily resist but would have no allies. Prague and other Czech cities could be destroyed by German aerial bombardment. The end result would be the same. Thus, the Czechs signed the agreement.

Hitler became the undisputed master of Germany. The German generals, who had distrusted Hitler, were overpowered by admiration for his commanding gifts. They now felt chagrined for their previous distrust of Hitler. {1-78}

On his return to London, Chamberlain addressed the cheering crowd, "This is the second time there has come back from Germany to Downing Street peace with honour. I believe it is peace in our time." {1-79} Churchill, though, took a different tack: "For the French government to leave her faithful ally, Czechoslovakia, to her fate was a melancholy lapse from which flowed terrible consequences. Great Britain, who would certainly have fought if bound by treaty obligations, was nevertheless now deeply involved, and it must be recorded with regret that the British Government not only acquiesced but encouraged the French Government in a fatal course." {1-80}.

After the meeting in Berchtesgaden, which was the first meeting with Hitler regarding the Sudetenland, Churchill observed the British and French cabinets. He concluded: "The British and French Cabinets at this time presented a front of two overripe melons crushed together; whereas what was needed was a *gleam of steel.*" {1-81} Military analyst, Raymond Aron, observed: "In every conflict a distinction has to be made between trial of force and **test of will**." Napoleon also believed, "War is not only a clash of physical resources but of character and will." (1-82)

Winston Churchill suggested that World War II should have been named "The Unnecessary War." (1-83) Nevertheless, more than 50 million people died in World War II. (1-84) These war dead could readily be attributed to the weak resolve exhibited by Britain and France in their negotiations with Adolf Hitler.

CHAPTER 2

BATTLES

Winston Churchill declared, "Great battles won or lost, change the entire course of events, create new standards of values, new moods, new atmospheres, in armies and in nations, to which all must conform." (2-53)

Battle of Sadowa

On October 31, 1517, Martin Luther, a Catholic cleric, nailed his now famous *95 Thesis* on the door of the castle church at Wittenberg, Germany. His theses were written in Latin that sought certain improvements within the Catholic Church. Unknowingly to Martin Luther, his thesis fanned the smoldering embers of reform within the church. Eventually a horrific war, The 30 Years War, evolved in Western Europe. It was fought between 1618 and 1648, and was deemed a religious war.

Catholic France, Austria, and Spain fought against Protestant Denmark and Sweden. However, Catholic France fought against Catholic Austria to keep Austrian power out of North Germany. The war was fought entirely on German soil. Consequently, the German population was reduced from 21 million to 13 million, as starvation was widespread. At the Treaty of Westphalia, which ended the war, Germany was divided into some 300 separate entities. These entities were ultimately divided along religious lines. The North German entities were Protestant while the South Germans were Catholic

Germany remained divided essentially the same until Napoleon invaded Germany in 1806. {2-1} Napoleon set about to reduce the number of German principalities to 39. This act improved Germany's goal toward unification. One German state, Prussia, rose above an insignificant status to a prominent position in Germany. Through marriage of the ruling classes and conquest, Prussia became a European power. Austria, though, was still the stronger power among the German states.

Although the German states had no single dominate state, they did form a German Confederation. It usually met in Frankfurt and was called the Diet of German Confederation. The lesser German states expressed a loyalty to either Prussia or Austria; Berlin or Vienna; Hohenzollern or Hapsburg.

Most Germans at the time wanted a unified Germany. Indeed, {2-2} Germans had desired unification since the 17th century. Cross-border customs and postal concerns were enough to bring about a union. Moreover, French emperor Napoleon III added impetus to German unification. Napoleon III wanted to annex the German provinces on the left bank of the Rhine River. (2-3) Only a united Germany could stand up to France. Catholic Germans in South Germany wanted union with Austria while Protestant North Germans wanted union with Prussia.

Austria, although a German state, had an empire that contained many non-German people. Austria's main interests were its possessions along the eastern Danube River. Its interests also included the recently acquired states from the defunct Ottoman Empire. Austria, though, did not want a strong Prussia that may become a future adversary.

Fortuitously, Prussia recognized that it had an adroit statesman, Otto von Bismarck. Bismarck might have been a skilled chess player, for he had the ability to foresee an opponent's move and perceive an opponent's reaction to his move. In order to create a united German state under Prussian leadership, Bismarck knew he had to go to war. First, it was Denmark that held the German provinces of Schleswig-Holstein. In this war, Prussia was successful.

Next, Prussia had to go to war with Austria. Austria for its part wanted to punish Prussia. Austria intended to partition Prussia and restore the German Confederation and enlarge Austria's German allies: Saxony, Bavaria, Wuerttemberg, Hess, and Hanover at the expense of Prussia. (2-4)

War was the only way to convince the German Confederation to join Prussia in its quest for German unification. The only south German kingdoms that joined Prussia were Baden and Luxembourg. All north German states, though, joined Prussia. The Prussian Army was then ordered to enter Saxony, Hesse, and Hanover. The war officially began on June 18, 1866. (2-5)

Austria, at the time, was at war with Italy and had a large force in the south. Thus, the Austrians could not meet the Prussians with all their forces. Nevertheless, the Austrians had 250,000 men to meet the Prussians with 256,000 men. The Prussians were advancing from the north. The Austrian commander, Field Marshal Ludwig Ritter von Benedek retreated and decided to make a stand at Sadowa, a town in the present-day Czech Republic.

Although, the two opposing armies were approximately equal numerically, there were differences. The Prussian infantry was equipped with the new Dreyse breech-loader rifle or needle-gun while the Austrians used the older Lorenz muzzle-loaded and riffled muskets. The rate of fire from the Prussian rifle was five times that of the Austrian musket. The Austrians planned to overcome this disadvantage with the bayonet. A mass of men at close ranks with fixed bayonets marching straight at their enemy is a terrifying sight. This tactic, though, would be fruitless against the superior Prussian fire power. The Austrian tactic was applicable in the prior century. Massed infantry marching shoulder to shoulder became outdated in the face of rapid fire from an enemy with advanced weapons. Moreover, the Prussian infantrymen fired their needle guns from the prone position, which provided them with protection and concealment.

The Austrians, on the other hand, were more effective with their artillery than the Prussians. The Austrians had 736 rifled, muzzled loaded cannon and 58 smooth bore guns (2-6) while the Prussians could field 492 rifled, breeched loaded cannon and 306 smooth bore guns. (2-7)

The biggest difference between the two armies was experience. The Austrians learned a hard lesson in 1859 when they engaged the French Army in Italy.

At the time, Italy was divided roughly into three parts. In the South, the Kingdom of The Two Sicilies, was paramount. In the middle the Papal States ruled while in the North, Lombardy or Piedmont was a separate entity and controlled by Austria. Piedmont sought independence and enlisted French support. At the Battle of Solferino, French artillery concentrated their fire on a selected area of the Austrian positions and then followed-on with swift charging French infantry.

Although the Austrian guns were inferior to the Prussian breech loaded guns, their artillery fought brilliantly in each engagement with the Prussians. In the end, the Austrian artillery effectively covered the retreat of the Austrian Army and saved it from destruction.

The Prussian artillery on the other hand had seen little action in the war with Denmark in 1864. The artillery was relegated to the rear of marching columns, and when the enemy was engaged, only a few guns were brought forward. Most of the guns stayed in the rear with the reserves. After the battle, a Prussian general, Prince Friedrich Karl, commander of the Prussian First Army, was heard to say, "The artillery was scarcely of more use than it could have been at Berlin."{2-8}.

Another difference between the two armies was their composition. All Prussian soldiers were German while only 40 percent of the Austrian Army was German. The majority of Austrian soldiers were Slavs {2-9} who were indifferent to the outcome for the mastery of Germany.

The Austrian Army was commanded by Field Marshal Ludwig Ritter von Benedek and was subdivided into seven corps. Benedek elected to hold defensive positions near the town of Sadowa in northern Bohemia. The Austrian commander was deemed brilliant, but many of his subordinate corps commanders were amateurish and incompetent. Thus, Benedek became depressed at the prospects of an Austrian victory.

Benedek knew he had to do battle with the Prussian commander, General Helmuth Karl Bernard von Moltke, who was aggressive and was prepared to gamble. The Prussian force was composed of three armies: First Army with 115,000 men, {2-10} the Second Army with 93,000 men, and the Army of the Elbe with 48,000 men. Initially the three armies covered a front of 260 miles {2-1} Moltke realized the Prussians were too widely dispersed and ordered all three armies to converge on the town of Gitschin in Bohemia.

The First Army and the Elbe Army arrived at Gitschen and confronted an Austrian unit whereupon it was dispatched. The Second Army, though, had not left its starting point. The telegraph system that Moltke relied upon had failed and the Second Army never received its orders. Moltke observed, {2-12} "No plan survives the first contact with the enemy." The Second Army was thus separated from the other two Prussian Armies, a very dangerous position for the Prussians. Moltke then signaled the Second Army to march to the sound of the guns. The Second Army then marched to the main battle area but encountered the Austrians in two separate skirmishes. The Needle Gun, however, empowered the Second Prussian Army to pull through . . .

From these encounters, the Austrians must have been aware of the positions of the three Prussian Armies. The Second Army with 93,000 men was isolated from the other two Prussian Armies. Here was an opportunity for the Austrian Army to attack the Second Prussian Army and destroy it in detail. The Austrian Army outnumbered the Prussian Second Army by a ratio of two to one. While attacking the Prussian Second Army, the Austrians could screen the other Prussian forces with their very effective artillery and some cavalry units. Here was Austria's opportunity for total victory.

While waiting for news of the Second Prussian Army, the King of Prussia, Wilhelm I, asked General Moltke what arrangements had been made for a possible withdrawal. {2-13} Moltke, standing next to the king replied, "Here there will be no retreat. Here we are fighting for the very existence of Prussia."

The Austrian commander, Benedek, did not have confidence in his army's ability to maneuver on such a large scale. In addition, he was aware of the consequences of the Prussian's needle gun. His senior staff officers advised him to retreat to save Vienna. Instead of attacking the Prussian Second Army, Benedek ordered a retreat south to a position near the fortress of Koeniggraetz. The Prussian First Army and the Army of the Elbe began to attack the new Austrian position on July 3, 1866. Intense fighting began at 8:00 a.m. By 2:00 P.M... {2-14} the Prussian Second Army arrived and attacked the right flank of the Austrian Army. The battle was over. Benedek ordered a full retreat by 3:00 P.M... Austrian casualties were 43,000 men while Prussia had 9,000 casualties. At the Treaty of Prague, {2-15} which ended the war, Austria agreed to exclude itself from German affairs and recognized Prussian dominance of the North German confederation.

Battle of Sedan

The Battle of Sedan was one of many battles in the Franco-Prussian War, 1870-1871. It was, indeed, the decisive battle. The Franco-Prussian War was precipitated for the most nugatory reason. In mid-1870, Prussia tried to place a Hohenzollern prince on the Spanish throne during the time of a vacancy in the Spanish succession. Napoleon III, the French emperor believed this act threatened France with a two front war.

Further, he believed the French Army was invincible {2-16} and that a war with Prussia had to be inevitable. British historian, Sir Michael Eliot Howard, observed, {2-17} "By a tragic combination of ill-luck, stupidity and ignorance France blundered into war." Therefore, on July 15, 1870, France declared war on Prussia.

The French population was enthusiastic about a war with Prussia. Everywhere the people sang the *Marseillaise* and shouted {2-18} *A bas la Prusse!* and *A Berlin!* The people were confident in their leader, Napoleon III, the nephew of Napoleon Bonaparte. France under Napoleon III was militarily impressive in the Crimean War; the Italian campaign; the Mexican campaign and the Algerian campaign. These campaigns, though, were fought at some distance from France and French security was never in doubt. (The campaign in Italy was in the Piedmont where France supported the Kingdom of Sardinia in the war with Austria.) A war with Prussia would put French survival at risk, as France and Prussia shared a common border.

Notwithstanding, the French Army was prepared for war. It was armed with the breech-loading chassepot rifle and the mitrailleuse, an early type of machine gun. The chasspot rifle was superior to the needlepoint rifle in accuracy and rate of fire. (2-19) The French artillery, though, used the more inferior muzzle-loaded rifled guns. Moreover, the mitrailleuse was employed as artillery. The mitrailleuse was mounted on a gun carriage like an artillery piece.

After the war with Austria, the Prussians realized their inefficient use of artillery. Prussian artillerists became the butt of the Prussian Army. In the war with France, however, Prussian artillery was near the front with the infantry and many times in the front of the infantry. Moreover, all Prussian guns were superior rifled, breech-loading cannon.

The marked difference between the two armies was their preparation. Prussian mobilization proceeded smoothly. General Moltke used the railroads to bring the Prussian Army to assembly points. The South German States that were loyal to Austria in the war with Prussia now joined Prussia in the war with France. The Catholic South German States sided with Catholic, but German, Austria in the war with Protestant Prussia. In this war, ethnic loyalty of the South German States overrode their loyalty to the Catholicism of France. Prussia mustered 430,000 men. {2-20}

French mobilization was utter chaos. {2-21} Many reservists that were called to assembly points found that there were no uniforms for them, and others had no weapons. Officers could not find their units. Generals had maps of Germany but none of France. There were shortages of ambulances, canteens, baggage wagons, munitions and other supplies. The French Army call-up should have exceeded 385,000 men, but through incompetence, some 250,000 men were available. {2-22}.

The Prussian forces were divided into three armies. The 1st Army was under General von Steinmetz. The 2nd Army was under Prince Frederick Carl, and the 3d Army was under the Crown Prince Frederick William. General Moltke, the overall Prussian commander, anticipated a French attack, as France initially declared war. The attack, though, was not forthcoming.

The French Army was organized into six corps. Marshal MacMahon commanded the 1st Corps; Frossard the 2d; Bazine the 3d; Ladmirault the 4th; Douay the 5th, and Canrabent the 6th. France planned an offense across the Rhine near Strasbourg. {2-23} This strike was to affect a separation between North and South German states. However, through lack of organization and other short comings, the offense never materialized. {2-24}.

Meanwhile, the Prussian plan was to attack the enemy wherever he found him. After a series of major defeats, three French corps under the command of Marshal Bazaine retreated to the fortress city of Metz, which was then besieged by the Prussians. The bulk of the French Army under Marshal MacMahon was ordered to relieve the besieged French forces at Metz. Moltke, though, ordered the Prussian Third Army to intercept MacMahon and drive his forces away from Metz. The Prussians met MacMahon's French troops, which were driven away from Metz. MacMahon then retreated to the city of Sedan. The Prussians had no difficulty tracking MacMahon's forces, as the French newspapers gave a daily disposition of French Army units. {2-25}

The French forces under MacMahon at Sedan numbered about 130,000 men. The Prussians then set out to surround the town and place it under siege. The Prussians brought-up some 600 breach loading guns. {2-26} Breech loading guns had the capability to fire more rapidly than the older muzzle loading guns. Sedan, itself, was set in a valley and surrounded by hills. The Prussian artillery was placed on these hills and fired down upon the French troops in the valley. A French soldier was heard to say, *"Nous sommes dans un pot de chambre et nous y serons emmerdes." ("We're in a chamber pot* and we're going to be shat on.") {2-27} *The Prussian guns had a greater range than the French guns.* This placed

France in an inferior position, as the French guns could not carry out counter battery fire. The French forces at Sedan were in a 'mouse trap' {2-28}. The French forces attempted to break out but were repulsed. The Prussian artillery bombarded the French positions throughout the day and repelled every French attempt to escape. The French chasspot rifle and *Militareuse* amounted to little in the battle. Nevertheless, French General Emmanuel F.de Wimpffen urged the emperor to stand at the head of his troops and make one last charge. {2-29} Napoleon III declined, and all French forces at Sedan surrendered.

The Battle of Sedan did not end the Franco-Prussian War, but it was the decisive battle. It was only a matter of time for the French government to recognize the end. Napoleon III abdicated; the Second French Empire ended with the proclamation of the Third Republic. Prussian troops eventually placed Paris under siege. A peace treaty was signed at Frankfurt in February 1871.

The Franco-Prussian War united Germany for the first time. Germany now had a national anthem, *Deutschland Ueber Alles* (Germany Over All). The anthem was intended to unite Germany. Germans would no longer think of themselves as Bavarian, Saxon, Rhine Lander or Pomeranian Etc. but German. . . . . .

Battle of Stalingrad

A battle fought more than a half century ago still weighs heavily on the military attitude and ultimately the political position of a nation. On June 22, 1941, the German dictator, Adolf Hitler, launched "Operation Barbarossa," the plan for the German military invasion of the Soviet Union. Hitler envisioned a blitzkrieg campaign that was to require no more than four months. By year's end, the German Army was deep inside Russia, but victory was nowhere in sight.

The following year, 1942, Hitler opened a new offensive in the East to be carried-out by two Army Groups, each with a different objective. Army Group A was to advance south, cross the Don River and capture the Russian oil fields in the Caucasus area. Army Group B was to advance east toward the great port city on the Volga River, Stalingrad.

The German Army, at the time, did not have the strength to carry-out two major offensives simultaneously. The logistical problems alone should have overridden the plan. The German Chief of Staff, General

Franz Halder, did protest but then was relieved by Hitler. The German Army was set for a disaster. This was particularly evident by the divergent objectives of the two Army Groups: they could not assist each other. The military axiom, "Divide and conquer," was totally ignored by Hitler.

Hitler had faith in intelligence reports: *Foreign Armies, East*. The reports stated that the Red Army had no significant operational reserves. {2-30} Actually, they supported Hitler's own beliefs, "Ivan is finished."(2-31) The chief of German intelligence on the Eastern Front, Lieutenant Colonel Reinhard Gehlen, contended that the Soviet Army had a manpower reserve of 1,700,000 men in late 1942. However, since the Soviet Union comprised such a vast area, these forces could not easily be brought to bear on the Eastern Front. {2-32}

Army Group B was composed of the German Sixth Army; one corps from Fourth Panzer Army and auxiliary troops from Italy, Hungry and Romania. The auxiliary troops, which had inferior training and equipment, were to guard the flanks of the Sixth Army. In turn, the Sixth Army would provide the main assault force of Army Group B.

The thrust toward Stalingrad began on June 28, 1942. The Sixth Army encountered little resistance from the Red Army in its drive toward Stalingrad. Some Russian units attempted to impede the Sixth Army but were quickly dispatched. By November1942, the Sixth Army had captured 90 percent of Stalingrad. The Russians held four small enclaves on the left bank of the Volga River.

The University of Pennsylvania history professor, Thomas Childers, {2-33} observed that the German Army had breadth but little depth. A prolonged war in Russia required an army of considerable depth. The distance between Moscow and Berlin was about 1,000 miles. The Russian front between Leningrad and the Crimea was another 1,000 miles. Indeed, the Eastern Front was more than 2,000 miles long. A battle front is never a straight line. Pockets and bulges exist all along the line. Consequently huge gaps existed in the line that were left unguarded by German troops. The German generals had reason to be concerned with the "unfavorable ratio of force to space."{ 2-34}

The two offenses carried-out by the two Army Groups created two huge bulges in the battle line and extended its length another 300 miles. The flanks of these bulges were vulnerable, if not inviting, to an attack. The auxiliary troops protecting the flanks not only had poor equipment and training but also low morale. Morale is a key factor in every military unit's fighting capacity. If morale is high, men will fight with their teeth and bare hands if necessary.

A component of Soviet Military Doctrine is to allow the enemy to spend itself to near exhaustion and then attack him with hidden reserves. {2-35} Most Western Armies would send their reserves to support their besieged forces. This strategy would minimize casualties and impede the enemy advance. The Russians, on the other hand, were only concerned with destroying enemy forces. Their own casualties were of no consequence.

On November 19, 1942, the Red Army launched Operation Uranus that attacked the Northern flank of German Army Group B with three armies. The following day, November 20, 1942, the Red Army launched Operation Mars, which attacked the Southern flank of Army Group B. The two flank attacks by the Red Army were brought about by a Strategic Reserve force of 800,000 men. {2-36} .0

The Red Army did not directly attack the German troops in Stalingrad, but attacked only the auxiliary troops on the flanks of the German Sixth Army and then cut their supply routes about 50 miles west of Stalingrad. On November 23, 1942, the two Red Army flanking forces linked-up near the town of Kalach-on-Don. (2-37) The Red Army then proceeded to form two encircling rings around Stalingrad. The outer ring was formed to prevent a German relief force from entering Stalingrad. The inner ring was to prevent a German break out from Stalingrad. About 300,000 German and allied troops were thus encircled. {2-38}

The German General Staff realized that a relief force must be formed to save the German Sixth Army. Supplies, though, could be flown-in by the Luftwaffe, the German Air Force, and overland by armed convoys. By December 19, 1942, the overland relief force, the Fourth Panzer Army commanded by General Hoth, drove within 30 miles of the siege perimeter. {2-39}. In order to save the German Sixth Army, the encircled army had to fight its way to the German relief force. This action would thus abandon Stalingrad to Stalin. Hitler would have none of that. Hitler contended that the relief force was to support the Sixth Army by holding "Fortress Stalingrad" as designated by Adolf Hitler. (2-40)

The relief program by air would require the Luftwaffe to fly-in 750 tonnes of supplies per day. (2-41) Reichsmarschall Hermann Goering, the head of the Luftwaffe, said it could be done. However, the commander of the German Fourth Air Fleet and responsible for the Stalingrad sector, General Wolfram F von Richthofen, a cousin the Red Baron, believed otherwise. (2-42) He could only obtain enough aircraft to fly-in 300 tons per day. This amount, though, could only be realized under ideal conditions. Winter conditions and Soviet air defenses made flying over Stalingrad extremely hazardous. On November 24, 1942, 47 German planes attempted to fly to Stalingrad. Twenty-two of the planes were shot down. {2-43} The Luftwaffe continued to fly to Stalingrad but delivered only about 10 percent of the required supplies.

The Red Army for its part tightened the rings around Stalingrad. On December 24, 1942, units of the Red Army captured the Stalingrad airport. {2-44} The airport was the last vestige of hope the German Army at Stalingrad had of joining the main German Army west of Stalingrad. General Hoth's relief force, the Fourth Panzer Army, was driven back to its starting position by the Red Army.

To add to the misery of the besieged German soldiers was a system of loud speakers installed throughout the city by the Red Army. The speakers repeated a recorded message that sounded like the ticking of a clock: "tick-tick, -tick tick, every eight minutes a German soldier dies in Russia."

The German Army at Stalingrad continued to battle the Red Army; even though food, medicine, ammunition, fuel and morale were all but depleted. On January 20, 1943, the commander of the German Sixth Army, Friedrich von Paulus, sent the following message to the German High Command in East Prussia: {2-45}

COMBAT CAPABILITY OF TROOPS IS SINKING FAST IN VIEW OF CATASTROPHIC SITUATION WITH REGARD TO FOOD, FUEL, AND AMMUNITION. HAVE 16,000 WOUNDED WHO RECEIVING NO CARE WHATSOEVER. WITH EXCEPTION OF THOSE ON VOLGA FRONT, TROOPS HAVE NOT SUITABLE POSITIONS MORALE IS SINKING. ONCE AGAIN I REQUEST FREEDOM OF ACTION IN ORDER TO CONTINUE RESIST AS LONG AS POSSIBLE OR CEASE MILITARY ACTIVITY IF CANNOT BE CONTINUED, WOUNDED CANNOT BE CARED FOR AND TOTAL DEMORALIZATION AVOIDED.

The German High Command in East Prussia replied:

CAPITULATION IS OUT OF THE QUESTION. ARMIES ARE
FULFILLING THEIR HISTORIC OBLIGATION IN ORDER BY
STAUNCH RESISTANCE TO MAXIMUM TO FACILITATE
CREATION OF NEW FRONT AT ROSTOV AND WITHDRAWAL
OF CAUCASIAN ARMY GROUP

Hitler was aware of a German Army tradition: A German Field Marshal had never surrendered. Therefore, Hitler promoted General von Paulus to Field Marshal on January 30, 1943. Paulus surrendered on February 1, 1943. According to German sources, 318,000 German and allied troops were encircled in November 1942. Of these 29,000 were flown out to safety; 166,000 were killed in action, and 123,000 were taken prisoner. (2-46)

The debacle at Stalingrad could have been avoided had Hitler grasped that the battle for Moscow was a prognostication of the war in the East. The climax of the Battle for Moscow occurred one year, almost to the day, before the Battle of Stalingrad.

On September 30, 1941, the German Army began encirclement operations of Moscow. By mid-November, the German Army was 40 miles from Moscow. However, the severe Russian winter began to take its toll. The temperature dropped to -40 degrees Fahrenheit, and the German soldiers were still wearing summer uniforms. The plunging temperatures caused the guns not to fire and the tank engines not to start. The German Army was stretched to its limits, and the German soldiers reached the point of exhaustion. The German generals at the battle front realized that Germany would not defeat the Soviet Union by the end of 1941.

The German generals, nevertheless, had only a limited voice to remonstrate against Hitler's demands. On May 21, 1935, Germany passed a law whereby: "The Army was to be subordinated to the supreme leadership of the Fuehrer (2-47) Every soldier took the oath, not as formerly to the Constitution, but to the person of Adolf Hitler. The War Ministry was directly subordinated to the orders of the Fuehrer." The oath, which was given by every soldier, and included officers, read as follows, [2-48] "I swear to you, Adolf Hitler, as Fuehrer and Reich Chancellor, loyalty and bravery. I vow to you, and those you have named to command me, obedience until death, so help me God."

The oath was given with the tacit understanding that an officer will continue to follow his code of conduct. An officer's code stipulates that his first duty is to accomplish his mission. His second duty is to look after the welfare of the men he commands. The German General Staff expanded this last duty to include the welfare of Germany. The General Staff was non-political, but it was like a sturdy pillar within the government that most Germans fully perceived. When the German generals took the oath to Hitler, they assumed that Hitler, as leader of the German people, endorsed the officer's code. Corporal Hitler, though, was not mindful of the officer's code.

Hitler instead followed his own code: Triumph of the Will. In 1934, Hitler authorized the making of a very inspirational film, titled, *Triumph of the Will (Triumph des Willens)* The film was directed by Leni Riefenstahl and was something like the power of positive thinking but taken to an enhanced level. Hitler believed that if one held a strong conviction, the power of the will could surmount any obstacle notwithstanding the limited odds of success. Logic and strategic considerations were completely ignored. The power of the will could overcome any challenge. A German soldier armed only with a bayonet could triumph over a Russian soldier in a T-34 tank if his will were strong enough. If one did not triumph, then his will was weak and thus deserving of the punishment meted out by his adversary.

At the battle of al-Alamayn, Egypt, Field Marshal Rommel, the commander of German and Italian forces in Africa received the following message from Adolf Hitler on November 3, 1942: {2-49} "It is with trusting confidence in your leadership and the courage of the German-Italian troops under your command that the German people and I are following the heroic struggle in Egypt. In the situation in which you find yourself there can be no other thought but to stand fast, yield not a yard of ground and throw every man and every gun into the battle. Considerable air force reinforcements are being sent to C-in-C South. The Duce and Commando Supremo are also making the utmost effort to send you the means to continue the fight. Your enemy, despite his superiority, must also be at the end of his strength. It would not be the first time in history that a strong *will* has *triumphed* over the bigger battalions. As to your troops, you can show them no other road than that to victory or death."

When Germany annexed the Czech Sudetenland in 1938, Hitler and his generals inspected the abandoned defenses constructed by the Czechs. "Hitler's generals were appalled at their strength and told him they could not have taken them. 'It's not the guns but the men behind them,' Hitler replied" (2-50)

On December 6, 1941, the Red Army launched a massive counter attack to relieve Moscow. {2-51} One hundred fresh divisions from the Far East region were mobilized and sent into battle. These divisions were released from the East where they were guarding against a possible Japanese attack. The Soviet spy system under the master spy, Sorge, revealed that Japan intended to attack the U.S. and not the Soviet Union. (One day later, the Japanese attacked Pearl Harbor, Hawaii.) .

The German generals, aware of their perilous position before Moscow, wanted to fall back to prepared positions farther to the west, Hitler overruled them and gave the order to dig-in, which happened to be the correct order at the time. {2-52} "It seems to be almost an article of faith among military historians that this was Hitler's finest hour, the one enduring testament to the power of the *will* over and above mere strategic considerations."

At that moment, moreover, Hitler should have realized that his venture into Russia was a failure and seek a political solution. The German Army was scheduled to defeat the Soviet Army by the end of 1941. The Soviet Army was undefeated and now on the offensive. The German Army, though, still held the upper hand. This should have given Hitler political leverage to negotiate a favorable peace. In 1918, the German Army forced the then Red Government to sign a peace treaty at Brest Litovsk, Poland.

The German Army was trained in the war of maneuver and sought quick victories. The Red Army, on the other hand, was trained for a war of attrition by using steamroller tactics that would wear-down the enemy. The impasse before Moscow meant that the Russians would now command the battlefield, and Germany would now have to fight on Russian terms or a war of attrition. More significantly at the time, the German casualties had reached 800,000 men. The Barbarossa invasion force had been about 3.2 million men.

Hitler, though, believed that his will was triumphant by giving the order to dig-in, while his generals wanted to retreat. He now believed that he was a military genius and his generals were incompetent. This view proved devastating to the German Army and the German people. After the battle for Moscow and until the end of the war, over two million German soldiers died in Russia, and several million more left Russia permanently maimed.

One more casualty and equally destructive was the lost trust in the German Army and the German government by young Germans after the war had ended. Young Germans were not aware of the hold Hitler held over the officer corp. Nevertheless, the officer corps was responsible for the welfare of the German nation, and it should have overruled any allegiance to Hitler. When asked about rearmament, young Germans responded with the slogan of *ohne mich*, without me.

After the battle of Moscow, the German Army suffered one defeat after another. The defeats, though, were more akin to catastrophes. Nevertheless, Hitler would never change his battle concept: Triumph of the Will, and he would never accept another perspective. Finally, some senior German officers realized that Hitler would lead Germany to ruination unless they took action to eliminate him. In July 1944, some German officers attempted to assassinate Hitler, but the plot failed.

CHAPTER 3

WINNERS AND LOSERS

WARFARE HAS PROVED too crude and brutal for civilized people to espouse. Yet, it is the only means available to settle difference between nations. The League of Nations and the United Nations were organized to settle differences between governments and avert war. These organizations had noble convictions, but ultimately they were failures. Thus, a civilized nation at war must provide its own rules of war and set an example for others to follow.

In every conflict, a skillful commander attempts to accomplish his mission with a minimum number of casualties and loss of equipment. Since the world began, many battles have been fought. Only a few show a clear distinction between the winner and the loser. Four battles that show a clear distinction are described here. There are many others.

Battle of Sidi Barrani, Egypt, September 1940 to December 1940
Winner: British Western Desert Force
Loser: Italian Tenth Army

In 1939, the German Army invaded Poland, which precipitated World War II. Britain and France allied themselves against the Axes Powers of Germany and Italy. Benito Mussolini, the Italian dictator, was eager for the spoils of war and the return of Italy to the glory of ancient Rome.

Mussolini saw his opportunity in North Africa. Across the Mediterranean Sea from Italy was the Italian colony of Libya. Libya bordered Egypt which held the Suez Canal, the fertile Nile delta, and the storied cities of Cairo and Alexandria. Mussolini had 250,000 soldiers in Libya and believed that force could easily destroy the small British force in Egypt. Mussolini wrote Hitler, "preparations for an attack on Egypt with vast objectives are now complete." {3-1}.

The overall battle area was in North Africa, specifically two countries: Egypt and Libya. At the time, Egypt was a protectorate of Britain and Libya was a colony of Italy. A significant facet of the war in North Africa was the 1400 mile coast road that ran along and parallel to the Mediterranean Sea. The coast road defined the battle area. A commander may have dispatched a unit south of the coast road, but the unit was always used to support the main thrust, which was along the coast road.

The commander of the Italian Tenth Army, Marshal Rodolfo Graziani, was familiar with desert fighting. He had fought against the Senussi, an Arab tribe in Libya that rebelled against Italian rule. {3-2} The desert was barren, featureless and almost void of water. Logistical problems were almost unsurmountable, especially for the huge 250,000 man Tenth Army. A German general described the military conditions in North Africa, "a tacticians's paradise and a quartermaster's hell." {3-3}

War in the desert imposed its own special rules: Rule number one: Armies brought everything that they needed with them. They could not anticipate getting anything off the march. Consequently, the most precious items carried were gasoline and water. Rule number two: The importance of total mobility. In the desert, the infantry did not march. They rode in trucks. The queen of battle was the tank. Rule number three: The need for speed. A fast-moving, quick reaction army was required for victory in the desert. {3-4}

On September 13, 1940, the Italian Tenth Army left its advanced staging base at Sidi Omar, Libya and marched east toward Egypt. On September 16, the army reached Sidi Barrani, 65 miles inside Egypt. Here, Marshal Graziani ordered the army to halt and prepare defenses around Sidi Barrini. This was an incredible order, as Britain had only a nominal force in Egypt. In June 1940, most of the British Army had barely escaped destruction at Dunkirk, on the Northern coast of France. Most of the British Army, some 300,000 men, was evacuated from Dunkirk but had to leave their weapons behind on the French beaches.

British forces in Egypt, at the time, were commanded by General Sir Archibald Wavell. These forces, though, numbered only about 86,000 men. {3-5} With this force, General Wavell was directed to not only protect Egypt but also the Sudan, East Africa and the oil-rich lands around the Persian Gulf. {3-6} General Wavell also had to be mindful of the 350,000 Italian troops in Eritrea, East Africa, south of Sudan and a possession of Italy.

After the catastrophe at Dunkirk, it would seem that Britain would retreat within itself. Defend the Home Island at all costs! Britain, though, had a powerful navy that could fend off an amphibious attack and believed it could risk sending much needed military supplies, tanks and guns to General Wavell. {3-7} Upon arrival of this military equipment, General Wavell ordered his staff to prepare plans for an offensive against the Italians at Sidi Barrani. {3-8}.

Ten days later, General Wavell's operations officer, Lieutenant General Richard O'Connor's plan was approved. The plan was code named Operation Compass and was to be set in motion on December 7, 1940. General O'Connor's force would have only two complete formations: the Fourth Indian Infantry Division and the Seventh Armored Division. The British forces would be outnumbered ten to one. Surprise, though, was a key element in the plan.

In November, troops participating in Operation Compass began training exercises. The troops attacked dummy "enemy camps" that resembled exactly Italian fortifications around Sidi Barrani. The enemy camps had previously been photographed by the Royal Air Force. Operation Compass proceeded on schedule.

Instead of attacking Sidi Barrani directly from the east on the coast road, General O'Connor initially attacked Nibeiwa, a fortified village south of Sidi Barran. Surprise was complete. British artillery began shelling Nibeiwa at 7:00 a.m. December 9. The Royal Air Force struck with every plane that would fly and dropped bomb loads on fortified camps and the forward airfield. {3-9} Simultaneously, British warships, off the Mediterranean coast, bombarded Sidi Barrani with heavy shells.

The Nibeiwa camp was then assaulted by British Matilda infantry tanks that were supported by the Fourth Indian Infantry Division. In two hours the Nibeiwa camp was in British hands. The British assaulting force then turned north to attack Sidi Barrani from the south. The next day, the remainder of the Italian camps around Sidi Barrani was overrun or was abandoned.

General Wavell continued the offensive. On December 16, 1940,

British troops reached the Libyan frontier. The only Italian troops in Egypt were in British prisoners of war camps. The Tenth Italian Army virtually ceased to exist. A British officer radioed headquarters, "We are guarding about five acres of officers and two hundred acres of other ranks." {3-10} British casualties were about 500 men. {3-11}

The Italian fiasco prompted Mussolini and Hitler to agree to send German troops to Africa. As a result, German General Erwin Rommel was selected to lead a German force to assist the Italian Army in Africa. On February 16, 1941, General Rommel was advised that he would lead two German divisions: the Fifth Light Division and the Fifteenth Panzer Division. These divisions would be known as the German *Afrika Korps.*

After some experience fighting alongside the Italian forces in Africa, General Rommel was able to ascertain the weakness of the Italian Army. He concluded that the Italian Army in Africa was designed to fight a colonial war against insurgent tribesmen. {3-12} The armored vehicles and tanks were too light and their engines under-powered. The guns used by their artillery units were from the first world war and had a short range. The army had too few antitank guns and anti-aircraft guns. Its rifles and machine guns were obsolete and unsuitable for modern warfare.

Above all, the Italian infantry was not motorized. {3-13} In desert war, non motorized infantry can only be effective in the defense of prepared positions. If a breakthrough occurs, though, the non motorized infantry would be too slow to converge on the breakthrough. Thus, the whole defense position would be in danger of collapse. . .

General Rommel was particularly horrified to learn that there were three scales of rations for the Italian Army in Africa. {3-14} One for officers; one for noncommissioned officers and one for other ranks in sharply descending order. When British troops overran an Italian camp, they found fresh bread, vegetables, canned ham and wine. They concluded that the Italian Army was the best-provisioned army that fought in the desert. {3-15} Unknowingly, they had come onto an Italian Officer's rations.

When Julius Caesar, one of the world's most successful military commanders, was on a military campaign with his troops, he ate what they ate. He slept on the ground wrapped in a blanket as they did. He slept in a tent if a tent was available for all his men. {3-16} Caesar set the example for successful commanders. By eating the same food and sharing the same sleep accommodations he would know by personal knowledge the fighting capability of his men.

General Rommel continued, "The gravest results of the Italian defeat were to their morale. The Italian troops had, with good reason, lost all confidence in their arms and acquired a very serious inferiority complex . . . Psychologically, it is particularly unfortunate when the very first battle of a war ends with such a disastrous defeat . . . It makes it very difficult ever again to restore the men's confidence." {3-17}

Battle of Inchon, South Korea, September 15, 1950 to September 28, 1950.
Winner: United Nations Forces (Mostly American)
Loser: North Korean People's Army

After winning the Russo-Japanese War (1904-1905), Japan annexed Korea. It remained a part of the Japanese Empire until World War II. At the Cairo Conference (December 1, 1943), Korea was promised its freedom by the Allied Powers.

One of the Allied Powers, the Soviet Union, had signed a non-aggression treaty with Japan in April 1941 and it would expire in April 1946. In April 1945, the Soviet Union advised Japan that it would not renew the treaty. {3-18}. From this, Japan concluded correctly that the Soviet Union intended to attack Japan.

Stalin, the dictator of the Soviet Union, advised the Western Allies that the Soviet Union would go to war against Japan three months after the end of the war in Europe, May 9, 1945. True to his word, the Soviet Union entered the war against Japan on August 9, 1945. This date coincided with the dropping of the second atomic bomb on Japan. The Soviet Union launched an overland attack from Siberia and drove east through Manchuria and Northern China. The Japanese forces opposing the Soviet troops were no-match for the more experienced and better equipped enemy. Though, Japanese troops continued the fight until Japan's format capitulation on September 2, 1945.

Since the Soviet Union entered the war against Japan, it could take part in the treaty ending the war. One of the minor parts of the treaty was the taking of Japanese prisoners of war. The United States and the Soviet Union made a hurried agreement on taking Japanese prisoners of war in Korea. They set-up an arbitrary line, the 38th parallel in Korea, as the dividing line to take prisoners. The Soviet Union would take

Japanese prisoners north of the line and the United States would take all Japanese prisoners south of the line. {3-19}

At first, there was little friction between the Soviet Union and the United States. Shortly after the surrender, however, the Soviet Union made the 38th parallel a political boundary, and the Iron Curtain dropped along the 38th parallel. For two years the United States went before the United Nations to present the case for Korean freedom and independence. The Soviet Union refused to cooperate.

Consequently, the Republic of Korea was established in the southern portion of Korea on August 15, 1947. {3-20} Its capital was Seoul. The Soviet Union declared this action illegal and set up a Communist puppet government in the northern portion of Korea and named it the Democratic People's Republic of Korea. Its capital was Pyongyang.

Further, the Soviet Union organized a North Korean Army. This army of 130,000 men was trained and equipped by the Soviet Union. The army included a brigade of Russian T-34 tanks, combat aircraft and a trained reserve force of 100,000 men. The North Korean Army included 25,000 combat veterans who fought with the Chinese Communists against the Chinese Nationalist in Manchuria. (1946-1948).

By contrast, the Republic of Korea Army had 100,000 men that were more of a national police force than an army. It lacked artillery, tanks, combat aircraft and reserves. The fighting strength of the two armies decidedly favored the North Korean Army.

On June 25, 1950, The North Korean Army crossed the 38th parallel in four columns. The invasion was a complete surprise. The North Koreans advance south met little resistance. The South Korean Army was not up to the task. The North Korean Army planned to take Seoul and the whole South Korean peninsula. The Communists would then possess all of Korea and the world would be forced to accept this as a *fait accompli.*

The United States had a few under strength divisions in Japan. These troops were sent to Korea but could only slow the advance of the North Korean Army. Ultimately, the United States was able to draw American troops from other areas and establish a defense perimeter around the port of Pusan in the southeastern part of the Korean peninsula. Possibly, Pusan was the only good port in Korea,

In addition to the United States military forces, fourteen other nations sent armed forces to support the United Nations' effort. The United Nations requested that President Truman name an American officer to command the troops from the fifteen nations. President Truman named General Douglas MacArthur for this assignment on July 7, 1950. {3-21}

General MacArthur set out to stabilize the Pusan defense perimeter. The defending forces had now become the Eighth Army and commanded by Lieutenant General Walton H. Walker. The North Korean Army continued attacks on the defense perimeter. However, the United Nations naval and air force attacked the North Korean Army's line of communications and gave close air support to the ground troops.

Four days after the North Korean invasion, General MacArthur observed the Korean battlefield. and concluded that the South Korean Army could not defeat the enemy on the present battlefield even with American reinforcements. However, he believed the North Korean Army could be defeated decisively by landing troops behind the North Korean Army and cut their lines of supply.

The port of Inchon was considered to be a good location to launch an amphibious invasion. Inchon was near the capital, Seoul, and more than 200 miles from the Pusan perimeter. Some members of the planning staff believed Kunsan, about 100 miles west of Pusan, would be a better choice. A landing at Kunsan, though, would not favor a condition to severe the North Korean supply lines. A Kunsan landing would be more of a diversionary attack to draw North Korean troops away from Pusan. This action would only prolong the war and not end it as General MacArthur stressed.

Inchon, though, was not ideal for a military operation. It was probably the worst of all harbors for an amphibious invasion. The approaches to Inchon were two narrow passages: Flying Fish and Eastern channels. These channels could easily be blocked by mines. The currents in these channels were three to eight knots, which made landing operations hazardous. Probably the worst flaws in the Inchon plan were the 32 foot tides that limited landing operations to a few hours a day. Landings could only be made during high tides. After the tides went out, only mud flats remained, which would impede military operations. Naval Commander Arlie G. Capps noted, "We drew up a list of every natural and geographic handicap, and Inchon had 'em all." {3-22} At a briefing, Admiral James Doyle concluded, "The best I can say is that Inchon is not impossible."

Surprise, training, and disinformation created conditions for a United Nations success. The invasion plan was code named: Operation

Chromite. About a week before the invasion, seven intelligence specialists were sent to a small island at the mouth of the channel, 10 miles from Inchon. From this location, the reconnaissance team relayed information about tides, mud flats, sea walls and enemy fortifications. One of the most important contributions was the relighting the light house on Palmi-do near Inchon, which would aid navigation for UN ships.

With the aid of a small group of civilians, the reconnaissance team deliberately spread information around Inchon and Seoul that the main invasion would be at Kunsan, a harbor farther south on the Korean Peninsula. As a result, only a small North Korean force was sent to Inchon. .This force, though, arrived too late to be effective.

In addition, a series of drills and tests were performed elsewhere on the Korean coast where conditions would be similar to Inchon. These drills were used to test the performance and timing of the landing craft. The invasion plan was then complete. However, the "Fog of War" has always interfered with best laid military plans.

General MacArthur was recognized as a towering figure among American military commanders. He was taking a huge risk to his reputation if the Inchon invasion failed. There were many reasons that it could fail. Every military plan does not always follow exactly the proposed schedule. His subordinate commanders may have failed in many ways because of unforeseen circumstances. A typhoon, which was not seen in a weather forecast, could unexpectedly strike Inchon at the time of the invasion. A landing group could miss the incoming tide and then forced to wait for the next tide. General MacArthur, the commander, would ultimately be responsible.

At the time of the Inchon invasion, General MacArthur was 70 years old. He knew the risks, but he knew his duty. Top generals in the Pentagon believed the Inchon landing posed too great a risk. General MacArthur, though, was able to allay their fears. Nonetheless, early in the amphibious operation, an erroneous report was sent out stating that the invasion was a failure. General MacArthur agonized for an hour before the correct report read, "whole operation proceeding on schedule."{3-23}

Two days before the amphibious operation, September 13, the Inchon harbor was bombarded by the guns of four cruisers and five destroyers. An aircraft carrier provided aircraft that struck violently at North Korean defenses. These attacks alerted the North Koreans that an attack at Inchon was imminent. Their reaction came too late. Lead elements of an UN landing force hit a beach in the Inchon harbor at 6:30 a.m. on September 15. On the evening of September 18, the U.S. Marines were at the edge of Kimpo air field, six miles from Inchon.

The UN forces were now in a position to cut the North Korean supply lines that were feeding North Korean troops around the Pusan perimeter. The North Korean Army was forced to retreat and was no longer a threat to South Korea. The Inchon landing was accomplished at a cost of 300 UN casualties while only 30 were killed in action.

Hostage Rescue Operations
Winner: Israel Defense Forces at Entebbe
International Airport, Uganda July 3-4, 1976
Loser: American Armed Forces at Desert
One, Iran April 24-25, 1980

Early in the morning of June 27, 1976, the Athens Airport routinely loaded and offloaded passengers. Scant attention was paid to any of the passengers. At 6:45 a.m., June 27, 1976, Singapore Airlines flight 763 landed at the Athens Airport. Of the five disembarking passengers, four proceeded to the Air France terminal. On the same morning at 8:59 a.m., Air France flight 139 left Ben Gurion Airport, Israel bound for Paris, France via Athens, Greece.

At Athens, Air France flight 139 released 38 passengers and added 58 new passengers. As they passed through customs and other inspections, the new passengers were not required to pass through a metal detector. A guard watching a fluoroscope paid scant attention to the screen.

At 12:20 P.M., Air France 139 was airborne and bound for Paris. The plane held 246 passengers including 104 Israelis and Jews. At about 12:30 P.M., the plane was skyjacked by some of the passengers carrying guns and hand grenades. The plane was then diverted to Benghazi, Libya.

At the Benghazi Airport the plane was refueled, and after seven hours it was again airborne. At 3:15 a.m., June 27, 1976, the plane landed at Entebbe International Airport in Uganda.

At the Uganda Airport, the passengers were taken off the plane and placed in the Old Terminal's transit hall. Here the skyjackers were identified. Eight were members of the Palestinian Liberation Organization and two were members of the Baader-Meinhof Gang, a German terrorist organization. Undoubtedly, the skyjackers were supported by the pro-Palestinian Ugandan President, Idi Amin.

The skyjackers then separated the Israelis and Jews from the other passengers. All of the non-Jewish passengers were permitted to leave as passengers on another Air France plane that was brought into Entebbe for that purpose. The Jewish passengers were threatened with death if Palestinian prisoners were not released from Israeli prisons;

Almost immediately after the Air France plane was skyjacked, responsible officials in Paris and Ben-Gurion Airport knew something was amiss, as the skyjacked plane lost radio contact. Shortly thereafter, they learned of the skyjackers demands.

The Israeli Government then decided upon a military operation to rescue the hostages. Two things favored the Israeli operation. The country adjoining Uganda, Kenya, was a bitter foe of the Amin regime. The building where the hostages were housed was built by an Israeli construction firm. The firm still had the building blueprints and passed them onto the Israeli government. From these plans, the Israelis built a partial replica of the building.

Israeli intelligence personnel interviewed the non-Jewish hostages in France. From these interviews, Israel was able to accurately determine a description of the building's interior, the number of terrorists, the involvement of Ugandan troops and many other significant details. The Israeli Defense Forces were now ready to plan the rescue operation. More than 100 Israeli troops including members of the elite Sayeret Matkal team trained and made ready for the raid. The assault was code named Operation Thunder ball/Thunderbolt.

Four Israeli Air Force Hercules transport planes flew from Israel and night-landed at 11:00 P.M. at Entebbbe Airport without the aid of landing lights or assistance from the Entebbe control tower. The Israelis then offloaded a black Mercedes automobile and several jeeps. The Mercedes and jeeps were loaded with Israeli troops and driven toward the terminal building. The Ugandan troops at the terminal were expected to believe that President Amin or other high Ugandan official was being escorted to the terminal. The Israelis succeeded in this deception.

The Israeli troops quickly jumped from the jeeps and attacked the Ugandan guards and terrorists. The raid was over in three minutes. Six terrorists and 45 Ugandan soldiers were killed. One hostage was killed and three later died. The remaining hostages were driven to Nairobi airport and flown back to Israel. Only one Israeli soldier was killed in the raid, He was the Israeli ground commander of the operation: Colonel Yonatan Netanyahu. Later the assault at Entebbe was renamed Operation Yonatan.

A little known story of the operation was the reaction of the French flight crew on Air France Flight 139. Flight Captain Michel Bacos, upon learning of the disposition of the Israeli and Jewish passengers at Entebbe, announced that all passengers on the flight were his responsibility, and he would not leave them behind. After hearing the flight captain's plan, the entire crew volunteered to stay with the captain and the hostages.

Another hostage rescue operation, Desert One, was carried-out by American armed forces. On November 4, 1979, more than 3,000 militant Iranian students stormed the American Embassy in Tehran and took 66 American hostages.

The action taken by the Iranian students was a reaction to American involvement in Iranian affairs. In the spring of 1979, the longtime ruler of Iran, Shah Mohammed Reza Pahlavi, was forced into exile by a popular uprising. After more turmoil, a Shiite Muslim cleric, Ayatollah Ruhollah Khomeni, took leadership of the country. Iran then became a theocracy.

Shortly after the Shah was overthrown, he sought medical assistance in the United States. The then President of the United States, Jimmy Carter, permitted the Shah to enter the United States. This permission triggered the Iranian student's uprising and the taking of American hostages. American diplomats attempted to have the hostages released but were foiled by Khomeini supporters.

The Pentagon then planned a rescue operation. The planners wanted a quick rescue effort such as parachuting an elite special forces team. Upon examining the environment in which the hostages were placed, the planners realized that a quick rescue was suicidal. The hostages were heavily guarded in the massive American embassy compound. The embassy was in Tehran, a city of four million people and surrounded by mountains and deserts. Intelligence information was unreliable and difficult to obtain.

After much deliberation, the Pentagon planners decided upon a two-night operation. The operation was code named: Eagle Claw. Preceding the two-night operation was the arrival of a 132-man U.S. Army team to Egypt's Wadi Kena on April 21, 1980. Three days later from this

Egyptian staging base, the team flew to Masirah Island off the coast of Oman. From Oman, the team flew to the advanced staging base, *Desert One*, which was in a remote location 200 miles from Teheran, Iran.

On April 24 at about 10:00 P.M., the team arrived at *Desert One*. Eagle Claw was on schedule. The next part of the plan was the arrival of eight RH-53D Sea Stallion helicopters to Desert One. These helicopters were to be flown from an aircraft carrier lying offshore in the Gulf of Oman. At Desert One, the helicopters were to refuel and then fly the team to a location in the mountains 65 miles southeast of Tehran.

On the following night the rescue team was to enter Tehran in four trucks, supplied by agents posing as Europeans. The rescue team planned to enter the embassy and free the hostages. The Sea Stallion helicopters were to fly into the embassy grounds and fly out with the hostages and the rescue team. From here the helicopters were to fly to an abandoned airfield, 35 miles outside Tehran. Army Rangers were scheduled to take possession of the airfield. Transport planes were to fly into the field and fly out with the hostages and the rescue team.

This was a daring plan. Surprise was essential for the plan to succeed. Timing was absolutely essential. The transport planes had to land at *Desert One* at night. The pilots had the use of night vision goggles, which was a new innovation at that time. A CIA operative had placed landing lights at *Desert One* and covered the lights with a light dusting of sand. The lights were to turn on from a remote station in the plane. The lights did turn on as planned and the transport planes landed safely.

The second phase of the *Desert One* operation was the anticipated landing at 11:30 P.M. on April 24, of the Sea-Stallion helicopters from the aircraft carrier. Prior to the helicopters arrival, however, a bus carrying 45 Iranian civilians blundered into *Desert One*. The Iranians were immediately placed in custody. Then a fuel truck and a pick-up truck drove into the area. The fuel truck was destroyed, as the driver refused to stop at a roadblock. The driver of the pick-up escaped. The Americans at Desert One began to question the remoteness of the staging area.

Desert One was scrutinized and determined to be a remote site with a favorable forecast of good weather. The Sea Stallions began to arrive but about two hours late. One of the Sea Stallions lost pressure on a rotor blade and was forced to land. It was abandoned and the remaining Sea Stallions flew onto *Desert One*. Before arriving, the Sea Stallions flew into a terrible dust storm, and one of the Sea Stallions lost the use of its gyroscope. It turned back. Upon landing, one of the helicopters discovered that its hydraulic pump had malfunctioned and could not take off.

Eight Sea Stallions left the aircraft carrier in the Gulf of Oman and flew to *Desert One*. A minimum of six Sea Stallions was required to complete the mission, but now, there were only five. Colonel James Kyle, the ground commander at *Desert One*, immediately realized that the mission could not be accomplished. He aborted the mission and ordered all aircraft and American personnel to leave *Desert One*.

After loading with American personnel, a transport plane was authorized to taxi out and take off from *Desert One*. Almost immediately, a Sea Stallion behind the transport plane lifted-off and banked toward the transport plane. The Sea Stallion struck the transport plane and burst into flames. Eight men on the Sea Stallion and transport plane lost their lives. *Desert One* was a disaster. The last plane left Desert One 30 minutes after the plane burst into flames. . . . .

Desert One was an American tragedy. Many brave men died. The ultimate tragedy, though, was the loss of American credibility. It exposed America's inept military operations. Military power and political power are almost inseparable. Indeed, Carl von Clausewitz, a recognized authority on war concluded; "War is continuation of policy by other means." {3-24}

CHAPTER 4

"FUSTEST WITH THE MOSTEST"

DURING THE AMERICAN Civil War, Confederate General Nathan Bedford Forest supposedly said, "get there fustest with the mostest." What he actually said was, "get there first with the most men." {4-1} Most people, however, prefer the more colorful speech. Nonetheless, he defined military logistics.

Baron Antoine-Henri de Jominni, strategic theorist and a staff officer under Napoleon, contended that logistics determined the military campaign. {4-2} On September 1, 1939, the German Army invaded Poland. In March 1939, Britain and France had guaranteed Polish sovereignty and on that account, declared war on Germany on September 3, 1939. The declaration of war was only symbolic, as Britain and France could not directly support Poland. Germany had complete control of the air and sea lanes plus overland routes to Poland. Without the arrival of external logistic support, Poland was defeated in three weeks.

At the end of World War II, the United States, Canada and its European Allies formed the North Atlantic Treaty Organization, NATO. This organization has subsequently accepted five principles of logistics. These are: foresight, economy, flexibility, simplicity, and cooperation. British Field Marshal Archibald Wavell said in 1946, "A real knowledge of supply and movement factors must be the basis of every leader's plan; only then can he know how and when to take risks with these factors, and battles and wars are won by taking risks."{4-3}

Berlin Blockade

NATO was formed on April 4, 1949 which signaled the beginning of the "Cold War." {4-4}. About a year before the formation of NATO, the Soviet Union endeavored to test the resolve of the Western nations having troops posted in Germany. At the end of World War II, Germany was divided into four zones of occupation. Each of the major victorious nations: the Soviet Union, the United States, Great Britain, and France, controlled a part of Germany. Berlin, the capital of Germany, was also divided into four zones of occupation. Berlin held a unique position. It was located deep within the Soviet zone of occupation.

Initially, the U.S. policy on Germany followed the Morgenthau Plan, which was to reduce Germany's industrial capacity to 50 percent of its 1938 level. France and the Soviet Union agreed with this plan. Britain, though, opposed the plan but did not obstruct its implementation. Upon fulfillment of the plan, the Western powers began to understand that they had underestimated the effect of the German economy on the rest of Europe. After reading a report from Europe dated March 18, 1947, former President Herbert Hoover urged a change in occupation policy stating: "There is the illusion that the New Germany left after the annexations can be reduced to a 'pastoral state.' It cannot be done unless we exterminate or move 25 million people out of it." {4-5}

General Lucius D. Clay, the commander of U.S. forces in Germany, and the U.S. commander of the Joint Chiefs of Staff were concerned over the growing influence of Communism in Germany and the declining economy in Europe. Thus, in the summer of 1947, the US Secretary of State, General George Marshall convinced President Truman to rescind the Morgenthau Plan on "national security grounds." Afterwards, the Marshal Plan, which placed large sums of US capital available for European nations requesting it came into being. The Soviet dictator, Joseph Stalin, opposed the plan and forbade any county in the newly formed Cominform, the countries in Eastern Europe overrun by Soviet troops, from accepting the aid. Molotov, a Soviet statesman, called the plan: "dollar imperialism."

The US and Soviet economic policies began to differ and in time became totally separate. The US wanted to build Germany into the economic center of a stable Europe. The Soviet Union wanted to destroy Germany's capacity to wage another war.

The Western powers, Britain, France and the US, realized that they would have to rebuild the German economy without Soviet participation. Thus, the three zones of occupation were integrated into a threefold alliance. The integration of the three zones in the west part of Germany also included Berlin, which remained isolated in the Soviet zone.

The Soviet Union soon realized that the lack of cooperation with the West was a boon to their ultimate goal: World Communism. If the West made independent decisions, the Soviet Union could also make independent decisions. Molotov accurately concluded, "What happens to Berlin, happens to Germany, what happens to Germany, happens to Europe." The Four Power Allied Control Council, which administered the occupation of Germany, met for the last time on March 20, 1948. A Soviet representative was chairman of the council during March, and it was the chairman's responsibility to schedule future meetings. No future meetings were scheduled, which effectively ended the Four Power Allied Control Council. President Truman acknowledged, "For most of Germany, this act merely formulated what had been an obvious fact for some time: namely, that the four-power control machinery had become unworkable. For the city of Berlin, however, this was the curtain-raiser for a major crisis."

On June 12, 1948, the Soviet Union declared that the Autobahn between West Germany and Berlin was "closed for repairs."{4-6} On June 21, all barge traffic to Berlin was stopped. On June 24, all rail traffic between Berlin and the West was stopped because of "technical difficulties." The next day, the Soviets announced that they would no longer supply food from their sector to West Berlin. The ground routes to Berlin were never negotiated with the Soviet Union. It was generally assumed that since Berlin was deep in the Soviet zone, ground routes would be made available to transport goods to Berlin. The Soviets rejected this argument. At the time, West Berlin had a 35-day supply of food and a 45-day supply of coal. There were about 2.5 million people in West Berlin. The Soviets believed the West had no option but to leave Berlin.

General Clay immediately sized up the American position. On June 13, 1948, he sent a cable to Washington, D.C.: "There is no practicability in maintaining our position in Berlin and it must not be evaluated on that basis. We are convinced that our remaining in Berlin is essential to our prestige in Germany and in Europe. Whether for good or bad, it has become a symbol of the American intent."

General Clay proposed the military option to break the blockade. He believed that sending a large, armored convoy from West Germany to Berlin with orders to use force if provoked. President Truman along with Congressional consensus overrode this plan stating, "It is too risky to engage in this due to the consequences of war." However, to support the principle that the United States would not abandon Berlin, President Truman on June 28, 1948 ordered the US Air Force to send B-29 bombers to airfields in Britain. The B-29 was the bomber that dropped atomic bombs on Hiroshima and Nagasaki, Japan three years earlier in 1945. {4-7} In February 1946, George Kennan, an American diplomat in Moscow noted, "Soviet power was impervious to the logic of reason. It was highly sensitive to the logic of force." {4-8}

Although the Four Powers never negotiated ground routes to Berlin, they did negotiate air routes. On November 30, 1945, the Soviet Union made a written agreement that there would be three 20 mile wide air corridors from West Germany providing free access to Berlin. Finding a loophole in the negotiated agreements was the easy part. Finding the aircraft to supply Berlin was the hard part.

West Berlin's daily food ration required a minimum of seventeen hundred calories per person per day. To obtain this level would require 646 tons of flour and wheat; 125 tons of cereal, 64 tons of fat; 109 tons of meat and fat; 180 tons of dehydrated potatoes; 180 tons of sugar; 11 tons of coffee; 19 tons of powdered milk; five tons of whole milk for children; three tons of fresh yeast for baking; 144 tons of dehydrated vegetables; 38 tons of salt and 10 tons of cheese. Thus, a total of 1,534 tons of food per day was required. In addition, the city required 3475 tons of coal and other fuels for heating and generating electricity. The city had been getting electric power from the Soviet sector but was terminated at the beginning of the blockade.

At the time, there were two airports in West Berlin: Tempelhof in the American sector and Gatow in the British sector. The French sector did not have an airport, and France did not want to participate in the airlift. They believed Berlin was a lost cause. France was, at the time, involved in the Indochina War,

Initially, the airlift was expected to last only three weeks. Nevertheless, Britain and the United States mounted a maximum effort to supply Berlin. Britain was ahead in the airlift to Berlin, as they had been supporting their Berlin garrison by air. With additional aircraft added to their sector, Britain was able to supply 400 tons per day to Berlin. The United States had two squadrons of C-47 aircraft in Germany. They had the capacity to haul 300 tons per day to Berlin.

This quantity, 300 tons plus 400 tons, fell way short of the required 5,000 tons per day.

The United States and Britain realized that they required greater aircraft lift capacity. Britain increased their fleet to 150 C-47 aircraft and 40 of the Aero York which had a 10-ton payload. These additional aircraft would bring the British contribution to 750 tons of supplies per day. The United States sent two C-54 aircraft groups to Germany. These additional aircraft increased the lift capacity to 600 tons per day, far short of the required capacity. By July 1, additional C-54 aircraft began to arrive in quantity.

During the first week, the airlift averaged only 90 tons per day, but the second week, the airlift reached 1000 tons per day. The Soviets ridiculed the airlift saying, "the futile attempts of the Americans to save face and to maintain their untenable position in Berlin." It became clear that the Soviets did not intend to lift the blockade.

The United States then began to intensify the airlift effort. Lieutenant General William H. Turner, who had organized the airlift over the Burma Hump during World War II, became operational commander of the Berlin Airlift. He became commander of **Combined Airlift Task Force** at Tempelhof on July 27, 1948.

General Turner immediately instituted new procedures. Instrument flight rules would be in effect at all times regardless of visibility. Each plane planning to land in Berlin had only one opportunity to land. If the plane's approach to the field was off, the plane could not circle the field and try for another opportunity to land. The plane that missed its opportunity to land was directed to fly back to the base near Frankfurt. This latter procedure reduced accidents and delays.

The Soviet Union attempted to intimidate the airlift aircraft crews by various methods. After one year, Western air crews endured 733 incidences of Soviet harassments. One method was for a Soviet fighter to buzz the cargo aircraft and fire its guns in the air near the aircraft. They also released balloons in the flight corridors; fired anti-aircraft guns, though none of the shells struck an aircraft, and searchlights were shining on the aircraft. The Soviet Union gave no indication that they would discontinue the blockade.

The Western powers realized that the blockade would last more than their original assumption of three weeks. Now, they had to prepare for winter. During the summer, a lift of four thousand to five thousand tons per day was adequate. During winter, the lift would be required to add an additional six thousand tons of coal per day.

The West had sufficient aircraft but needed more runways. The U.S. added a six thousand-foot asphalt runway at Templehof and the British added a similar runway addition at Gatow. These additions were helpful but more runways were required for the winter loads. Fortunately, France began to support the airlift. The participation of France in the airlift at this time was crucial. French engineers proceeded to build a new and larger airport near Lake Tegel in the French sector of Berlin. The airport was built in less than 90 days. After the blockade ended, the airport became the Berlin-Tegel International Airport.

The daily volume steadily increased. By April 1949, the airlift supplies reached 8,893 tons per day. On April 21, a point was reached when the airlift supply was greater than the amount previously supplied by rail. .In May 1949, the Soviets conceded that the West would not abandon Berlin. Therefore, they lifted the blockade. {4-9} The airlift, however, continued until September 1949.

Nickel Grass

Another crucial airlift administered by the US occurred in 1973. On October 6, 1973, Egyptian, Syrian and a few Iraqi troops launched a surprise attack on Israeli positions in the Sinai and Golan Heights. The Sinai and the Golan Heights were captured by the Israelis during the prior "Six Day War," which took place between June 5 and June 11, 1967.

The surprise attack was launched at noon on October 6, 1973. This date held special significance to Arabs and Jews. For the Arabs, it was the tenth day of the Muslim month of Ramadan. This was the time when the Koran was revealed to Mohammed. For the Jews it was Yom Kippur or "Day of Atonement," which was the most sacred day of the Jewish calendar. It would also be the time when most Israeli soldiers would be permitted to leave their defense positrons and participate in spiritual rites. {4-10} This new struggle would be called the Yom Kippur/Ramadan War.

The Syrians opened their attack at 2:00 P.M. on the Israeli position in the Golan Heights, which were in Syria. The Syrian Front was relatively narrow compared to the Egyptian Front, which was along the Suez Canal. After "Six Day War," the Israelis created a defense line along the Suez Canal with bull dozers that pushed back sand making giant sand ramparts. The sand rampart was named the Bar Lev Line, which was named for the Israeli chief of staff, Ran-Alf Claim Bar Lev {4-11} The Bar Lev Line extended from Ceinture in the north to Port Tiphook on the Gulf of Suez in the south.

The Bar Lev Line was not intended to contain the Egyptian forces if they attacked but to determine if the attack were merely probing or an all-out assault. The Israelis would then know how much strength was needed to repel the attack. Having acquired the Sinai Peninsula in the Six Day War, the Israelis had the luxury of a defense in depth. Before this acquisition, Israel was a very small nation with a border difficult to defend. From the border with Lebanon in the north to Eclat on the Red Sea in the south, the length of Israel was only 265 miles. Near the city of Tel Aviv, Israel was only 12 miles wide. {4-12} Thus, the borders of Israel were its first and last line of defense. The Israelis had to be very sensitive about their country's borders with the Arabs.

This sensitivity was particularly evident during the Six Day War. A few weeks before the war, Soviet agents, who were allied with the Arabs, began to disseminate military information throughout the Arab world that the Israelis were amassing troops for a major attack against an Arab state. Egyptian Premier Gayal Abdul Nasser made warlike speeches against Israel. Later, Egypt ordered the UN peace-keeping units out of the Sinai Peninsula. {4-13} By May 23, the last UN peace keeper left the Sinai. Nasser then blocked the Gulf of Aqaba; so that Israel did not have access to the Red Sea and world commerce. The Gulf of Aqaba was considered international waters. A leader of the Palestine Liberation Organization, Ahmed Shukairy, exclaimed on June 5, "We will wipe Israel off the face of the map and no Jew will remain alive."

Instead of waiting for the Arabs to attack, Israel launched a preemptive attack on the Arabs. On the morning of June 5, 1967, about 180 Israeli military aircraft flew from their bases in Israel and disappeared over the Mediterranean Sea. They then flew well north and west of Cairo. and then turned about attacking Egyptian airfields from the west. Undoubtedly, the Egyptians watched for an attack from the east. The war was over with an Israeli victory. The outcome of the Six Day War was determined in the first three hours of June 5. {4-14} Without air support, the Arab armies were indefensible and unable to mount an attack. The Israeli Army had only to collect prisoners and enemy equipment. Israel also acquired the Sinai Peninsula, which was four times the size of Israel. {4-15}

The Egyptians and their Soviet advisers learned a hard lesson from the Six Day War. They would do better in the next war. They must act to neutralize the Israeli Air Force. Thus, the Egyptians and Syrians along with their Soviet advisers placed dense concentrations of antiaircraft missile sites, including surface to air missiles on the Suez and Syrian fronts. These included the radar-controlled ZU-23, the SAM-6 and the SAM-7. {4-16}

Another Egyptian innovation that was a complete surprise to the Israelis was powerful water cannons mounted on pontoons that washed away huge holes in the Bar-Lev sand rampart. The water cannons were more effective than the use of explosives. Through these holes, the Egyptian troops, tanks, and artillery pieces poured into the Sinai. The Israeli Air Force attempted to counter this invasion but was met with a hail of anti-aircraft and surface to air missiles. {4-17}

The Israeli ground counterattack suffered the same fate. Egyptian infantrymen armed with Soviet "Sagged" missile launchers, lay buried undetected in the sand, destroyed a large number of Israeli tanks. Israel lost half of its tank force on the first day of the war. The Egyptian Army advanced about 10 miles into the Sinai with little opposition. They then dug-in and set-up defense positions while bringing up their missile umbrella. {4-18}

The Israeli losses in the war were a third of its total combat aircraft or 102 planes. Also lost were 800 tanks and 300 armored vehicles. The number of military personnel killed was 1,854 with 6,000 wounded. {4-19} On October 9, Israeli Prime Minister Golda Meir issued a personal appeal for assistance. European nations absolutely refused, but the U.S. agreed to send aid and military supplies. U.S. President Richard Nixon was prompted to support Israel when he learned that the Soviet Union began a large scale resupply operation to support the Arab forces.

The first flights of U.S. aid arrived in Israel within 48 hours of the decision to act. The U.S. Air Force shipped 22,235 tons of tanks, artillery, ammunition and other supplies in C-141 and C-5 transport aircraft. The air shipments arrived between October 12 and November 14, 1973, and were critical to Israel's survival. The US airlift to Israel was called Operation Nickel Grass. A sea lift vessel also left the U.S., bound for Israel, carrying more equipment and supplies than the total of all the combined transport aircraft. However, the ship arrived 20 days after the hostilities began and 12 days after the cease-fire. {4-20}. This latter account corroborates Prime Minister Golda Meir's response of an American guarantee, "By the time you get here, we won't be here." {4-21}.

The airlift had to overcome certain political issues. The Arabs issued a warning that all oil shipments would stop to any nation that assisted Israel in its defense. The Europeans interpreted this warning to the extent to not allow U.S. aircraft to overfly their territory or land for refueling. Only Portugal was willing to help. Portugal permitted US aircraft to use its Lajes Airfield in the Azores. The Azores are located in the Eastern Atlantic Ocean and about 1,000 miles from the nearest major land mass. {4-22} They are directly west of the Strait of Gibraltar and, therefore, were an ideal advanced staging base for American aircraft landing on their first leg of the flight between the U.S. and Israel. Portugal's Lajes Field grew to house an additional 1,300 people. Soon more than 30 American aircraft per day were moving through Lajes.

Between the Azores and Israel, the American aircraft had to fly along precise routes over the Mediterranean Sea. They had to fly north of hostile Arab nations in Africa and south of European nations in the north. The U.S. Sixth fleet provided planes from aircraft carriers to escort the transport aircraft over the Mediterranean Sea. An aircraft carrier was posted every 600 miles in the Mediterranean Sea. When the transport aircraft were within 150 miles of Israel, fighters from the Israeli Air Force escorted the transport aircraft the remaining distance to Israel.

The American aircraft used in the airlift were the C-141 Starlifter and the C-5 Galaxy. The C-5 was particularly invaluable, as it could carry "outsize" loads. It carried the M60 Patton tanks, the M109 howitzers, mobile tractor units, and CH-53 Sea Stallion helicopters and many other "outsize" units. The American airlift continued until November 24, although the war ended on October 24.

The war ended with a decisive Israeli victory, but Egyptian President Anwar el-Sadat earned political prestige among the Arabs. At the outset of the war, the Egyptian Army forced the Israeli Army to retreat. Sadat, thus, achieved a great deal of respect for the Arab fighting man. In the Six Day War, the Israeli Air Force's support of ground troops made the victory in that struggle possible. In this war, moreover, the ground troops, tanks, infantry; and artillery, overran and destroyed Egyptian SAM sites that, in turn, freed the Israeli Air Force to attack without the hazard of flying through missile defenses. The Israeli Air force then became an effective arm as it was in the Six Day War. The Israeli Armed

Forces then trapped the 20,000 man Egyptian III Corps on the East Bank of the Suez Canal. {4-23}. This entrapment forced the Arabs to come to terms along with Soviet and American support.

First Gulf War

Another American logistic effort was performed in the First Gulf War that occurred between August 2, 1990 and February 28, 1991. This war was fought between countries bordering the Persian Gulf. Specifically Iraq accused Kuwait on the border with Iraq of stealing oil from Iraq through slant hole drilling. To compensate for this theft, the dictator of Iraq, Saddam Hussein, ordered the invasion of Kuwait. On August 2, 1990, Iraq's Amy of 120,000 men and 850 tanks crossed into Kuwait and then moved south to threaten Saudi Arabia, which was on Kuwait's southern border. If Iraq captured Kuwait and Saudi Arabia, they would have control of the majority of the world's oil reserves. Kuwait and the US immediately requested a meeting of the UN Security Council who passed Resolution 660 that condemned the invasion and demanded a withdrawal of Iraqi troops.

US, President George H. W. Bush decided to act and announced that the US would launch a "wholly defensive" mission named: *Operation Desert Shield*. On August 8, American troops moved into Saudi Arabia to prevent Iraq from invading Saudi Arabia. This defensive gesture had only a minimal effect on Saddam Hussein.

On August 8, Saddam Hussein announced that Kuwait was a province of Iraq, indicating that he had no intension of abandoning Kuwait. The US Navy then mobilized two battle groups comprising aircraft carriers USS *Dwight D. Eisenhower* and USS *Independence*. Two battleships were also sent to the region: the USS *Missouri* and the USS *Wisconsin*. The US Air Force sent 48 F-15 fighter aircraft to bases in Saudi Arabia and patrolled the borders with Iraq and Kuwait. The US Army began a military buildup that eventually reached 543,000 troops.

The UN Security Council passed several resolutions. The most significant was Resolution 678 that gave Iraq a withdrawal deadline of January 15, 1991. The US then assembled a coalition of countries to oppose the aggression of Iraq. Thirty-four countries joined the US to force Iraq to leave Kuwait. The coalition assembled 956,600 troops to engage Iraq.

The coalition forces required military equipment and supplies. Some of the major military equipment sent to the region was as follows: 3360 tanks, 3633 pieces of artillery, 4,050 armed personnel carriers, 1,959 helicopters and 2,600 fixed wing aircraft. Eighty-five percent of this equipment arrived by sea and 15 percent arrived by air. Almost all of the coalition's total military force of 956,000 troops arrived by air. That is, 99 percent of the coalition military personnel arrived by air. {4-23]

The military buildup for *Operation Desert Shield* began on August 8, 1990.. However, by October 1990, the buildup was still insufficient to have stopped an Iraqi invasion of Saudi Arabia had Iraq attempted an invasion. {4-29} Iraq simply allowed its enemy to build-up a staging base to attack it. A first rate military power would not permit this without sever harassment and interdiction.

A first rate power would attack the enemy ships with submarines, mines, aircraft and missiles. Iraq's principal strength was its army. It had a few small ships but could not challenge the naval power of the coalition naval forces. Its air force took refuge in Iran before the fighting began. It did have Scud missiles, which were fired more to terrorize the enemy than to inflict military damage. No Scud missiles were used to attack enemy supply depots in Saudi Arabia. It did attack an American military barracks in Dahran, Saudi Arabia, and 28 US soldiers were killed. Iraq also fired 39 Scud missiles into Israel inflicting extensive property damage. Three Israelis were killed and 78 were injured.

This latter attack could have derailed the coalition war effort. An attack on Israel always invoked an immediate retaliatory response from Israel. The US urged the Israelis not to retaliate, as this would make the war against Iraq an Arab-Israeli conflict. The coalition forces aligned against Iraq contained many Arab countries.

Operation Desert Storm, military operations, began on January 16, 1991, after the UN and Arab League passed resolutions regarding the conflict. Resolution 678, passed on November 29, 1990, gave Iraq a withdrawal deadline of January 15, 1991. Iraq ignored the deadline. The Coalition forces launched their attack at the Saudi-Kuwait border. Aircraft and artillery attacked Iraq military installations in Kuwait. Coalition infantry was deployed in forward staging areas that gave the appearance that they would attack at any moment.

The major ground attack, however, was launched at 4:00 a.m. on February 24, 1991 west of Kuwait in the Saudi desert. Some believed that this area would not support heavy tanks, as the tanks would be swallowed up by the soft sand. The tanks, though, crossed into Iraq from Saudi Arabia without impairment. As the desert had no road signs or other land marks, the coalition tanks used G.P.S. (global positioning system) to identify their location. The coalition's attack from the west put the right flank of the Iraqi Army in jeopardy. If this attack were not intercepted, the Iraqi Army in Kuwait could be cut off and defeated in detail.

Another detriment facing the Iraqi Army was the 100,000 man Turkish Army positioned on the Iraqi northern border with Turkey. The Iraqi Army was then forced to fight on three fronts: .Kuwait, the Coalition invasion force on its right flank, and Turkey on its northern border. Panic or "every man for himself" seemed to pervade the Iraqi Army especially the troops posted in Kuwait. These troops evacuated Kuwait and headed north on the main Kuwait-Iraq highway. The retreat was disorganized and proceeded without air defenses. Planes from the Coalition Air Force then swooped down on the retreating Iraqi Army. The road was then named "the highway of death."

As the Iraqis had no air force to specifically locate the enemy ground units, they had difficulty mounting a credible defense. Further, the Coalition Air Force kept the Iraqi army scattered and unable to concentrate ground units to mount an attack. Consequently, hostilities ended on February 28, 1991, at 8:00 a.m. After a 100-hour ground campaign, President Bush declared a cease fire, the day before, on February 27, 1991.

The Iraqi Army missed an opportunity to bring the war to a favorable conclusion. Not only did they not try to intercept the Coalition military buildup, but also failed to continue the attack into Saudi Arabia after occupying Kuwait in August 1990. The Iraqi Army consisted of 1,200,000 troops, 5,800 tanks, 5,100 other armored vehicles, 3,850 artillery pieces plus an elaborate missile and gun defenses. With this amount of strength, the Iraqi Army could readily advance south along the Persian Gulf and occupy the city of Dhahran, Saudi Arabia. This occupation may not have won the war, but it might have been enough to force the Coalition to accept a negotiated settlement. The Iraqi Army would not have had air support. Though, it would have shoulder-mounted antiaircraft guns and missiles. During Desert Storm, the Iraqi Army downed 75 Coalition aircraft with these weapons.

Above all, Iraq was not a first rate military power. Staff work was totally absent. In a future war, the US may not encounter such a helpless enemy. It must be prepared to fight a first rate power at a great distance from its shores. Complicating the US strategy is its position as the leader of the free world set between two huge oceans. Further, it has made many alliances in far-flung regions.

In the Pacific Ocean, the US has alliances with Australia, New Zealand, Taiwan, Korea and Japan. In the Atlantic Ocean, the US has an alliance with NATO, or North Atlantic Treaty Organization From its name the word Atlantic seemed to encompass the organization. The treaty was founded in 1949 and included Belgium, Canada, Denmark, France, West Germany, Greece, Iceland, Italy, Luxembourg, Netherlands, Norway, Portugal, Turkey, United Kingdom, and the United States.

Since the Cold War ended, NATO has expanded to include many countries formerly in the Soviet bloc. NATO must now include not only the Atlantic Ocean but also the North Sea, the Baltic Sea, the Mediterranean Sea, and the Black Sea as part of its organization. Further, as President Roosevelt declared in 1940, "We must be the great arsenal of democracy." {4-25} The US would, thus, be expected to send war materials and troops to any besieged country within the treaty organization. In 1934, Winston Churchill reflected on the Roman maxim, "Shorten your weapons and lengthen your frontiers." But the British maxim at the time was, "Diminish your weapons and increase your obligations." {4-26} This latter maxim could readily apply to the US today.

NATO has long realized that the Achilles Heel of its organization is its logistics system. The Atlantic and Pacific Oceans are wonderful defensive shields, but are onerous when trying to protect shipping lanes. The US has a strong navy, but it cannot protect all ships in the shipping lanes. During World War II, Britain had a strong navy, but England was brought almost to starvation in the spring of 1941 by German submarines attacking ships headed for England. {4-27} The indomitable Winston Churchill said early in World War II, "The only thing that ever really frightened me during the war was the U-boat peril." {4-28}

Today's submarines are much more advanced than the submariners of World War II. Submarines employed in World War II were all diesel electric. When submerged, the submarine operated on battery power, which required no air. When the submarine surfaced, it used its diesel engines, which require air as part of its fuel requirements. At the same time the surfaced submarine charged its batteries and propelled the submarine. The diesel electric submarines were also limited by the time and depth they could be submerged. The crews operating the submarines lived in an environment that was cramped, confined and reeking with a foul odor.

Today's submarines are nuclear powered and large enough to give the crews freedom to move about in a relatively clean environment. The submarines can submerge to greater depths and stay submerged indefinitely. The most significant technological advancement in a nuclear submarine is its weaponry. These submarines can be armed with missiles that have a range of 4,000 nautical miles. Each missile in turn can be fitted with 8-14 armed warheads that are independently guided. They can also be armed with underwater-to-surface missiles, that is, anti-ship missiles with a range of 35 miles which is three times the range of a torpedo. Besides torpedoes, the submarine can launch cruise missiles. {4-29} Today's nuclear submarines no longer need to visually see their target and moreover its enemy cannot visually see them. The nuclear submarine will probably be the capital ship of the next great war. In World War I, the capital ship was the battleship, and in World War II, it was the aircraft carrier.

At the end of the Cold War, Russia possessed the world's largest submarine force. Since then, this force was probably allowed to go to ruin. However, since the price of crude oil has increased at a phenomenal rate, Russia probably now has the economic resources to rebuild its submarine fleet. Russia is one of the world's largest oil exporters.

Russian submarine technology has made significant advances. Its newest class of attack submarine is identified as *Akula*, {4-30} which means shark in Russian. This class of submarine became operational in 1988 and it is believed that several such ships are now in service. This submarine incorporates the latest technology in quiet operations making the ship difficult to locate and attack.

The *Akula* is not the only serious Russian submarine threat. The Oscar {4-31}class submarine, which became operational in 1981, is considered by antisubmarine warfare crews to be the most dangerous threat to NATO carrier battle groups. The Oscar is not only armed with torpedoes, but is also equipped with twenty-four supersonic anti- ship cruise missiles with a range of 550 kilometers. Russia has several Oscars in service. The nuclear-powered Oscar-class submarine is an extraordinary ship. It is 150 meters long, which is much longer than a football field. From bow to stern this ship would have difficulty squeezing between the end zones of the Rose Bowl. Its submerged displacement is 16,000 metric tons. The most innovative feature of the submarine is its double-hull. The distance between the outer and inner hull is three meters. Water filled tanks are placed between the two hulls that provide excellent sound insulation. Moreover, the two hulls make an Oscar difficult to sink. Submarine experts claim that a minimum of three, standard Mk-46 air-launched torpedo hits would be required to sink an Oscar.

Another part of the Russian naval strategy is the use of mines. The Russians have stockpiled several thousand naval mines, which is the world's largest stockpile. These mines include deep water rising mines and underwater electric potential mines for use against submarines under ice. Mines are usually in defense service, but the Russians also use them in attack patterns. Russian submarines, surface warships, merchant ships, and fishing vessels plan to lay mines in the transatlantic shipping lanes. Mines will also be used against NATO's home ports to create a mine blockade. This will disrupt shipping and operational deployment of ships and submarines.

Russia is not our only potential adversary. China could readily become an antagonist. China wants Taiwan to be a part of China, and the US has a defense treaty with Taiwan. China possesses both nuclear and diesel-electric submarines for more than a total of 50 ships. Doubtless, China would employ more than submarines in a possible conflict with the US.

Now, a new vexing problem for the US Navy is the proliferation of diesel-electric submarines. It appears that some of the world's navies are turning back to World War II submarines. The new diesel-electric submarines, however, have advancements in technology, such as air-independent propulsion and fuel cells. These technological advancements have permitted the diesel-electric submarines to extend their operational ranges under water. {4-32} Once their fuel cells are charged, they can sail to the bottom of coastal waters and remain undetected for days. The diesel-electric submarines generate less noise than nuclear submarines and, therefore, are far more difficult to detect than nuclear submarines. The greatest danger from the new diesel-electric submarine is that they can be equipped with the Club anti= ship missiles. France and Russia have exported the new diesel-electric submarines to more than 39 nations. The latest number of diesel-electric submarinesowned by the various countries is 377 ships. Some of the nations purchasing the ships are: Algeria, China, Malaysia, Indonesia Singapore and Venezuela.

CHAPTER 5

FIRST STRIKE

FOR CENTURIES, COUNTRIES with surplus food production had the strongest armies and, therefore, usually defeated their enemies. Indeed, Napoleon was credited with the expression: "An army marches on its stomach." At the advent of the Industrial Revolution these criteria changed. Steel production became decisive. Countries with sizeable steel production then became strong military powers. Bismarck is noted for the expression: "Blood and iron."

In the atomic age, a still newer criterion of military power was created: nuclear weapons. At the close of World War II, the United States dropped two atomic bombs on Japan. For a few years thereafter the US was the sole possessor of nuclear weapons. In 1949, the Soviet Union broke America's monopoly on nuclear weapons. The nuclear genie was out of its box. To maintain America's lead in nuclear weaponry, President Truman then gave the go ahead to scientists to develop a hydrogen bomb. In 1952, the United States successfully detonated a hydrogen bomb. A year later, the Soviet Union also had a hydrogen bomb. Britain and France soon followed with their own nuclear weaponry. Scientists soon became aware that with rapid improvements in technology, many less formidable nations could fashion a nuclear bomb.

Nuclear war became a feared possibility. The whole of a nation's inhabitants could be slaughtered in minutes. This possibility broached not only new political positions but also psychological consequences. Man as an individual and as a species was forced to consider his ultimate existence. Self preservation, preservation of the species, and basic security, which had been taken for granted, became predominant.

Warfare took on a new meaning. Until the advent of nuclear weapons, war was denoted as simply war. No one attempted to distinguish between a little war, big war, short war, quick war, or prolonged war. Nuclear weapons forced man to deliberate about warfare, as man now had the capability of mass extermination. Great civilizations of the past have gone through a period of slow decline and eventual collapse, but none disappeared in a matter of minutes. National survival then became a paramount feature of war. Some limits had to be placed on warfare or nations could be annihilated in minutes. Thus, terms as *Limited War* and *General War* were adopted to describe man's involvement in the new age of nuclear weapons.

General War was the term to describe an all-out nuclear war. National survival would have been the paramount concern. On the other hand, *The Dictionary of US Military Terms for Joint Usage, Limited War* was, "Armed conflict short of general war, exclusive of incidents, involving the overt engagement of the military forces of two or more nations." Some like the military analyst, Robert E. Osgood, believed that the central characteristic of limited war was its limited objective; other analysts such as Bernaard Brodie maintained that restraint of the use of force was the controlling factor.

World War II was a limited war. America's goal was to disarm the enemy country and replace the regime. The United States Secretary of the Treasury during World War II, Henry Morgenthau, wanted to transform Germany into an agricultural, peasant society and to split the country into five different states. Such a policy, if followed, would approximate the definition of general war as national survival would have been an issue.

If a war must be fought, then a limited war is definitely preferred. Warring nations must be aware of the difference between a limited war and a general war. A limited war may escalate into a general war, but a general war cannot de-escalate to a limited war. To a certain extent the United States has attempted to avoid a general war by placing a limitation on one weapon system. The United States has unilaterally and totally renounced biological warfare. Such renunciation supports Bernard Brodie's definition of a limited war.

If a war is inevitable, then a limited war without nuclear weapons is the eternal hope of mankind. Even the smallest nuclear device must be removed from each nation's tactical and battlefield arsenals. Any nuclear device is still a nuclear weapon. Retaliation by a large nuclear weapon in response to a small nuclear weapon is too great a temptation.

During the early part of the Battle of Britain in World War II, about ten German bombers lost their way to military targets near Rochester and Thameshaven, and consequently, jettisoned their bombs over England. Unknowingly, they dumped their bombs on central London. Any British target would be better than bringing the bombs back to the home base. This error, nonetheless, led to an immediate British reprisal. On the next night, eighty British bombers bombed Berlin. This in turn led to reprisals by Hitler against London.

The great powers have recognized their vulnerability to nuclear war. Accordingly, and through trial and error, they have attempted to reconcile their nuclear capabilities. At the end of World War II, the only force keeping the Red Army out of Western Europe was the American nuclear arsenal. The United States and its NATO allies relied upon America's nuclear triad consisting of land-based missiles, sea-launched ballistic missiles, and manned bomber aircraft carrying bombs and cruise missiles. Only one of the triad segments was needed to destroy the Soviet Union; the remaining two were redundant yet a practicable part of the strategy. It fulfilled two major objectives. It forced the Soviet Union to implement three different defense systems, and it insured that if one segment were destroyed in a surprise attack, the surviving two segments could deliver a devastating blow onto the Soviet Union.

The nuclear triad strategy was called "massive retaliation" and was in place from the end of World War II until the Cuban Missile Crisis in 1962. The nuclear triad kept the Red Army at bay when the armies in the West were demobilized. In 1962, the Soviet leader, Nikita Khrushchev, was forced to back down during the Cuban Missile Crisis, as President Kennedy was able to give the Soviet leader unequivocal evidence that the United States had an overwhelming number of strategic nuclear weapons poised to strike at the Soviet Union. After this experience, the Soviet Union increased its strategic nuclear arsenal to not only match but also overmatch the American capability. The Soviet build-up effectively neutralized the American nuclear strategy of "massive retaliation."

The United States and the Soviet Union were forced to maintain a strong nuclear capability to insure that neither nation would gain strategic dominance over the other. America's nuclear triad thus became a preventive defense rather than an effective offensive arm. In 1967, the then Secretary of defense, Robert McNamara, formally introduced "flexible response" as the new NATO strategy. This strategy was also called a "graduated response" to a military threat. Initially, NATO was to respond with conventional weapons in the event of a Soviet attack. If the attack could not be so contained, then nuclear weapons were to be employed.

The United States and the Soviet Union, also made more formal efforts to reduce the chances of a nuclear holocaust. For many years, the two superpowers held Strategic Arms Limitations Talks or SALT discussions to reduce the number of intercontinental ballistic missiles or ICBM each nation held in its arsenals. These discussions moved forward slowly and with great caution until 1986, when the two heads of state met at Reykjavik, Iceland. There, caution was seemingly thrown aside. President Reagan offered to remove intermediate range nuclear weapons or INF from Europe. Reagan made this offer without first consulting with his European allies. This lack of consultation threw Europe into a trauma, as it showed that the United States was insensitive to Western Europe's vital interests, and it exposed Western Europe to its greatest vulnerability: warfare with conventional weapons. Providentially, no decision was reached at Reykjavik.

In June 1992, the Russian and American leaders agreed to a further reduction in nuclear weapons. They agreed to pare down their long range nuclear missiles or ICBM by two-thirds.

This agreement was a reversal of the West's military doctrine. At the inception of NATO, the only weapons holding the massive Red Army in check were nuclear-armed American ICBM.

Although the United States and the Soviet Union, which in a practical sense became Russia, reduced their nuclear weaponry, the world was not safe from nuclear war. Many other nations possessed nuclear weapons. Great Britain, France, China, India and Pakistan openly admitted owning nuclear weapons. Other nations are believed to be well on their way to developing nuclear weapons.

Many times the smaller nations see a need to possess nuclear weapons as a way to prevent intimidation and not as an action to initiate nuclear war. Nuclear weaponry has evolved from a pure military advantage to a political threat. Pakistan, for example, has nuclear weapons to offset the nuclear power of its neighbor, India.

Possessing nuclear weapons, though, does not necessarily constitute a nuclear power in the atomic age. A nation like a prize fighter must be able to take a punch. A prize fighter who has a "glass jaw" can never succeed in the fight game. Nations like prize fighters must be able to take a punch and then retaliate with a devastating blow. Without the capability to retaliate, no nation may call itself a nuclear power even though it may have stockpiled vast quantities of nuclear weapons.

Some suggest that Britain is a nuclear power as it possesses a large number of nuclear weapons. Britain, though, has a limited retaliatory capability. At one time, during a discussion between NATO leaders early in the cold war, one participant stated that three H-bombs were all that was needed to wipe the British Isles off the face of the earth. An indignant British general then rose to his feet and protested that it would take five H-bombs. Such a distinction is rather moot, as an attacker would probably launch many nuclear bombs.

A defender may resort to an ABM (anti- ballistic missiles) system, but these systems have been only partially successful. The Patriot surface-to-air missile system, a modest ABM system, which was used in the Gulf War, was only partially successful. A partial nuclear defense of Britain would be unacceptable.

The necessary, retaliatory capability can only be achieved by nations with large contiguous land masses and large populations. Only three of the world's nations possess these requirements: the United States, Russia and China. As yet, China is not the nuclear equal to Russia and the United States. China, though, is vigorously striving to achieve nuclear parity. There is no reason to believe that it will not succeed. Possibly, at a later date, India may fall into this group. No one will know for sure until India is put to the test.

Other nations with a large land mass such as Canada and Australia could not sustain a nuclear attack, as the populations of these nations are small and concentrated in specific areas that could readily be targeted. Their retaliatory capability would thus become improbable.

A new nuclear principle has then come into being: "First Strike." This principle implies the ability of one side to launch a nuclear attack against a nuclear armed opponent with such destruction that the enemies' ability to launch an effective counter nuclear blow will be destroyed. America's nuclear defense triad and extensive land masses make it virtually immune to "First Strike." Russia and in the near future, China are also immune to "First Strike." Because of their large land masses, multiple nuclear weapons, and large populations, these three countries will be the only states having this immunity.

Undoubtedly, China, Russia, and the United States would suffer grievously by a surprise nuclear attack. The enemy, though, would be unable to prevent a devastating nuclear retaliatory strike. The enemy nation would cease to exist. All forms of life would be destroyed. Every human being, animal, tree, and other forms of vegetation would disappear. Thus, any nation, other than the three immune nations, contemplating a surprise nuclear attack on China, Russia, and the United States must also contemplate its own ultimate destruction. The great powers, China, Russia, and the United States, therefore, hold an unequaled position in the atomic age.

The leader of Libya, Muammar Qadhafi, wisely said, "If you use a nuclear bomb, you are in effect using it against yourself." Subsequently, Qadhafi has removed all weapons of mass destruction from Libya's arsenal. {5-1}

At one time during the Cold War, US Secretary of Defense McNamara favored a minimum deterrence approach: All the US needed, in his view, was an arsenal that could ride out a Soviet nuclear attack and then respond strongly with nuclear weapons to destroy a certain percentage of Soviet industry, population and military might.

This proposal was countered by Secretary of Defense James R. Schlesinger who wanted a more credible strategy: He pushed for development of an arsenal better suited to attacking hardened Soviet silos, as opposed to soft targets such as cities. This strategy continued under President Carter and Defense Secretary Harold Brown who called it: "countervailing strategy." {5-2} Subsequently, a strategy of "Mutual Assured Destruction" or MAD was adopted.

The one thousand or so nuclear weapons possessed or soon to be possessed by each of the great nuclear powers guarantees their retaliatory capability. America's retaliatory capability is not only for America's protection but is also for the protection of its allies. During the Cold War, the United States provided a nuclear umbrella for its NATO allies in Western Europe and Canada. Thus, a nuclear attack on an NATO member nation was considered an attack on the United States. A retaliatory attack on the belligerent nation would then be swift and in kind. The United States with its nuclear triad of land-based bombers; land-based rockets in hardened silos, and sea launched ballistic missile submarines, which are mobile and concealed by the obscurity of the sea guarantees America's retaliatory capability.

Each of the great powers has enough nuclear weapons to destroy the world several times over. The nuclear weapons possessed by the three great powers, though, cannot be used to launch a nuclear war but only to guarantee retaliation against any nation with nuclear war in mind.

Nevertheless, there is no guarantee that a nation will not launch a nuclear attack against another nation. During the First Gulf War (1990-1991), Iraq had stockpiled great quantities of chemical weapons and had no reservation about using them. It had used chemical weapons in its war against Iran (1980-1988) and against its own people, the Kurds. Notwithstanding, Iraq did not fire a single chemical round against the Coalition Army advancing against it. In the last hours of the war in an act of desperation, Iraq might have fired all of its remaining chemical weapons at the conquering army. This act, though, could have produced an overwhelming chemical reprisal that would have engulfed all of Iraq. An axiom among chemical warfare professionals, "The best defense against chemical warfare is chemical warfare." Accordingly, a credible chemical warfare unit will dissuade an enemy from using chemical warfare as a weapon. Military analyst, Thomas Schelling, observed, "The threat of violence in reserve is more important than the commitment of force in the field." The threatened violence in reserve would not necessarily be chemical. It could readily be nuclear.

The world has witnessed enough nuclear devastation to create doubts about launching such an attack. Nuclear war is deemed so fearful that most people consider its horror beyond imagination. This very horror acts as a preventive. People all over the world are aware of the nuclear bombing of two Japanese cities during World War II. When the nuclear power plant in Chernobyl, a town in the Ukraine, collapsed in 1986, nuclear radiations fall out spread all over Europe for several weeks. Some 100,000 people had to be evacuated from an 18-mile radius around Chernobyl. Four years later, it was learned that the evacuation was too conservative, and an additional 200,000 people had to be cleared from the area. Nuclear authorities contend that an all-out nuclear exchange between Russia and the United States would destroy Europe, North America, and Russia. Such devastation would not accomplish the objectives of either nation.

The Russian word *sderzinvaniya*, which means restraining, may be applied to nuclear weapons. A reasonable consensus among the world's leaders has thus become, "The balance of terror has paradoxically become the bridesmaid of eternal peace." War, nonetheless, is not eliminated. Only nuclear war is deterred. Moreover, the United States must not be forced to use nuclear weapons because of inadequate conventional war capabilities.

Nevertheless, Russia and the United States each possess thousands of nuclear weapons readily on call. An accident due to carelessness or a deliberate act of a disgruntled soldier could create a situation ripe for nuclear destruction. Such a situation did occur a few years ago. While patrolling the Persian Gulf in 1988, an American cruiser, the USS Vincennes, which was equipped with the latest radar gear, accidentally shot down an Iranian airliner. One theory for the cause of the accident was a phenomenon called "perceptual bias," people see what they expect to see. The crew's bias was intensified by events that happened to a similar ship, the USS Stark. In May 1987 during the Iran-Iraq War in which the US provided Iraq intelligence support, an Iraqi aircraft fired on the Stark. The mistaken Iraqi aircraft attack resulted in killing 37 American crewmen. (5-3)

To lessen the possibilities of an accidental nuclear war, China, Russia, and the United States should store away all nuclear devices except strategic nuclear weapons. These latter weapons have sufficient safeguards to preclude accidental firing. Moreover, the strategic weapons have the inherent capability of deterring nuclear war, which are their huge warheads. This view was shared by President George H. W, Bush who, in 1991, ordered nuclear weapons carried by aircraft to be placed in storage. In March 1994, President Clinton announced an extension of the US moratorium on nuclear weapons testing through September 1995.

An interesting story that was only recently revealed occurred during the Cold War. The Soviet Union planned to carry out a First Strike nuclear attack on the United States. The attack was designed to circumvent America's early warning system. Early in the Cold War, the United States fashioned the "Dew Line" or Distant Early Warning Line. The line was composed of radar sites placed in Northern Canada to intercept Soviet bombers flying from the Soviet Union, over the North Pole and toward the United States.

Later, the ICBM, intercontinental ballistic missiles, was perfected, which precluded the need for aerial bombers. At the same time radar was also improved. The United States then installed three BMEWS radar sites, Ballistic Missile Early Warning System. These technically advanced radar sites were placed in Alaska, Greenland and an island off the north of Scotland. With this system in place, the US believed it would achieve at least 30 minutes advanced warning of a Soviet missile attack approaching over the North Pole, the shortest route from the Soviet Union. The Soviet Unions's first operational ICBM was the SS-6. When launched, the ICBM would rise to an elevation of 1,200 miles. A few minutes after the launch, the BMEWS would view it on its radar screen. The operators of the radar sites would immediately alert the Pentagon and other government leaders in Washington. DC The US could then launch a massive retaliatory strike with bombers, land-based missiles and sea-based missiles.

The Soviet Union was aware of the American plan. It then devised an alternate plan of attack that would make the American defense plan outmoded. Instead of attacking the US over the North Pole, attack over the South Pole. Also, when the missile is launched, do not let it rise more than 150 miles above the earth. With this system in place, the Soviets believed the US warning time would be reduced to a few seconds. The United States, in the 1960s, did not have radar with BMEWS capability guarding the southern approach. The Soviet Union named their new system FOBS or Fractional Orbital Bombardment System. The Soviets constructed 18 operational FOBS silos at a site near Tyuratam and activated its first operational unit on August 25, 1969.

Fortunately for the United States, FOBS was not a precision weapon. Its circular probable error was more than three miles. Therefore, it could not destroy hardened American ICBM silos. A Soviet attack with an FOBS would not be a First Strike effort, as it would not prevent an American retaliatory strike. Between 1969 and 1983, the Soviet Union had deployed FOBS rockets ready to strike the United States. In the 1970s, SALT, strategic arms limitation talks, was being reviewed. SALT II was signed in 1979. The treaty specifically mentioned the SS-9 FOBS as one system marked for deactivation. {5-4}

During the Cold War, the US had only to contend with a possible nuclear attack from the Soviet Union. Fortunately, the Soviet Union imploded and the Cold War ended. By coincidence, the Cold War ended at about the time the Twentieth Century ended. Now, in the Twenty-first Century a new type of war has plagued the United States: Islamic terrorism. This new type of warfare is in addition to a possible missile attack by China or Russia. If China or Russia launched a missile attack against the United States, the US would immediately retaliate with a missile attack of its own.

An attack by a terrorist organization against the US, however, may not trigger a retaliatory attack. A possible scenario: A freighter in the Atlantic Ocean approaches the American East coast and launches a missile armed with a nuclear warhead that detonates over a densely populated area. Millions of Americans are incinerated. The derelict ship is sunk, and its identity and origin are unknown. An American retaliatory attack cannot be launched, as the target nation cannot be positively identified.

The Islamic terrorists have also introduced a new dimension to their threat: suicide bombers. On September 11, 2001, Islamic terrorists flew aircraft into the Twin Towers in New York City. All people on board the aircraft were killed. Before the air crews boarded the planes, they knew they would be killed to accomplish their mission. This virulent attitude permeates Islamic terrorism. When people driving car bombs and individuals carrying bombs move into populated areas, they kill and maim hundreds of people. The lives of the bomb carriers are also lost, but they knew they would die. In 1979, Iran's Ayatollah Khomeini said, "I say let Iran go up in smoke, provided Islam emerges triumphant in the world." {5-5}

Furthermore, the United States must face another substantial threat: EMP, an electromagnetic pulse. To illustrate this threat, consider a possible scenario: A freighter in the Atlantic Ocean launches a nuclear armed missile that detonates 300 miles above Chicago, creating an EMP. Gamma rays scatter in what is called the Compton effect, and three separate pulses disable electronics and transformers. All devices dependent upon electricity are disabled. America would be thrown back to the early nineteenth century. Retaliation could not be fulfilled, as the enemy nation could not be readily identified. Western Civilization would be sent reeling.

Compounding the EMP threat to the United States is Iran's ability to launch ballistic missiles to set off an EMP. Recently, the Iranians have tested their Shahab-3 missile over the Caspian Sea in a way to set off an EMP. They have successfully launched two tests. It is believed that Iran has produced hundreds of Shahab-3 missiles. Iran's President Mahmoud Ahmadinejad declared in 2005, "Is it possible for us to witness a world without America and Zionism? But you had best know that this slogan and this goal are attainable, and surely can be achieved." {5-6}

CHAPTER 6

SALAMIS

A LITTLE KNOWN BATTLE fought in the Fifth Century B.C., determined the fate of Western Civilization. This battle, Salamis, was fought by two Greek City States against the Persian Empire. The Greeks were not aware that they were fighting to preserve Western Civilization. They were fighting to preserve their way of life. . . .

Today, the position of the United States in history is very much like the position of Greece about twenty-five hundred years ago. The American people are not aware that they were assigned the duty of preserving Western Civilization. Unfortunately, there is no other nation that can accomplish this undertaking.

Around 430 B.C., and as it does today, Greece occupied the southern tip of Europe. It had also, at the time, colonized parts of Spain, Italy, Turkey, North Africa and areas around the Black Sea. {6-1} Greece was separated from Asia by the Aegean Sea and the Hellespont, a narrow strait between Europe and Asia. It is one to four miles wide and 40 miles long. It is now called the Dardanelles.

During the Sixth Century B.C., a new force, Persia, began to sweep through Asia. Emperor Cyrus and his descendants conquered lesser kingdoms and added them to the Persian Empire. Persian rule required that all subjects within the empire must worship the king. They must also pay exorbitant taxes and support internal peace. The Persian king insisted upon the gathering of a diversity of cultures into political unity.

The Persians treated conquered people fairly. Conquered people within the empire became loyal to Persian rulers. This was the result of the Persian rulers' acceptance of the conquered people's culture and implanting decentralized governments. Above all, the people of Persia were protected from an invader by the strong Persian Army.

Greece, at that time, held an entirely different view. The Greeks worshiped no mere man, loathed paying tribute and enjoyed fighting small wars. The Greeks banded together in autonomous city-states where every citizen was known to all others. This culture supported their strongly individualistic life. Most of the city-states were in unending turmoil, as they tried all sorts of governments; but, above all, they were independent. The Greeks had a common language and a single unforced religion, which was absent among the Persians. Thus, the Greeks practiced political diversity within a common culture.

The independent minded Greek city-states were easy marks for the swelling Persian Empire. If the Greeks were united into a single nation, they could have better defended themselves. Consequently, the Greek city-states in Ionia, Thrace, and Boeotian fell to the Persians. The conquered city-states had little choice. If they did not surrender, their city would be plundered and burned and the inhabitants killed or cast into slavery. At the time, it seemed that all Greece would fall to the overwhelming might of the Persian Empire.

Athens, though, stood firm. The Athenians would not surrender their freedom for an ignominious life within the Persian Empire. Through conquest, Athens incorporated the villages around Athens, which increased the population of the Athens city-state. The conquered people were customarily treated as slaves. Instead, they were given full Athenian citizenship. Athens then made another bold step: no one could be enslaved for nonpayment of debt. Probably the most significant innovation was judicial assemblies were open to all citizens. Women, however, were barred from citizenship. Athens at the time, 500 B.C., had deviated from the course that was demanded by absolute ruled states. Athens was not a democracy as is known today, but democracy had been born.

Athens, located on the sea coast, became a city of sailors, traders, and merchants. It also became known as an armor manufacturer. Its armor gave military dominance to the hoplite, a heavily armed infantryman. Athens, also, depended upon every able-bodied male citizen between the ages of 18 and 60 for defense. Most Athenian males were able-bodied, as they spent part of every day in open-air "gymnasiums," boxing, running and wrestling.

To foment a problem for the Persians, Athens along with another city-state, Eretria, actively aided a revolt of the Ionians against their Persian masters. In the process, they laid waste an Ionian city. The Persian reaction was immediate. Persia sent an attack force across the Aegean Sea and attacked the city-state of Eretria. The citizens were slaughtered or enslaved.

Next, the Persians sailed down the coast to Marathon, a city part of greater Athens. About 10,000 Athenians and 1,000 men from the nearby city of Plataea took positions to oppose the invading Persians The Greeks were outnumbered by at least two to one. The Greeks sent a messenger from Marathon to Sparta to request military assistance. The Spartans replied that military assistance would be forthcoming from Sparta but only after they had completed religious festivities. Without Sparta, the Athenian Greeks were in a weak position.

Compounding the Greek position was the awareness of the Persian strategy. The Persians at Marathon were to draw away the Athenian army from Athens, leaving the city vulnerable to attack by a stronger Persian force sent by ship around Attica to Athens. After some discussion among the generals, the Greeks realized they must attack the Persians at Marathon and then reel about to defend Athens.

In battle, the Greeks favored the phalanx, a formation of hoplits carrying spears that were seven to 10 feet in length. {6-2} The phalanx was formed with men standing shoulder to shoulder followed by ranks eight to twelve deep. The spears of the first five ranks protruded beyond the first rank. An enemy facing the phalanx would then confront a mass of spear points

The plan of attack submitted by General Miltiades was accepted by the other Greek generals. The Greek plan was unorthodox, as they strengthened the flanks of their attacking force but left the center relatively weak. After this force was formed, the Greeks marched against the Persian positions. After they became within bowshot range, less than 200 yards, the Greeks began to rush the Persians' positions. The Persians moved against the weak Greek center, which was easily forced back. The Persian thrust, however, enhanced the Greek position. The two strong Greek flanking forces squeezed the Persians like a giant vice in a double envelopment attack.

The battle was over. The Persians, after leaving about 6,400 Persian dead, rushed for their boats. The Greeks lost 192 dead. General Miltiades then ordered his victorious army to march to the defense of Athens, some 26 miles away. Preceding the march back to Athens was the famed runner Pheidippedes who was sent by Miltiades to Athens to inform the citizens not to lose heart. The victorious Greek Army was on its way to Athens. Fortunately, the Greeks arrived in Athens before the Persian ships arrived. Upon seeing the Greek Army positioned to defend Athens, the Persians hesitated briefly and then sailed away. Belatedly, the Spartans arrived that evening to find that they had missed the fight. {6-3}

The new king of the mighty Persia, Xerxes, was infuriated by the upstart Greek city-states. Ten years after the Persian defeat at Marathon, Xerxes set out to conquer all Greece and end the Greek problem for all time. He assembled an army of 200,000 men, probably the largest force ever assembled at the time. This army was too large to live off the land. Therefore, Xerxes sent a naval force of 1,500 warships and 3,000 transport vessels to accompany the army. {6-4}

Most of the Greek cities believed Persian power was too strong to resist and elected to be neutral or join the Persians. Only Athens and Sparta plus adjoining villages decided to resist the Persians. Athens was a naval power and Sparta a land power. Thus, the two allies had differing concepts of defense. The Athenians requested the opinion of an Oracle who advised that safety was in wooden walls. This was interpreted as wooden ships or triremes.

A trireme was an Athenian warship with three decks, hence its name. It was 140 feet long and had a beam of 20 feet. {6-5} Its crew contained 170 rowers who manned 15 foot oars. The top deck had 62 rowers, the middle deck 54, and 54 on the lower deck. The ship was fitted with a rostrum, a 10-foot ram on the prow of the ship. The rostrum was used to drive holes into enemy ships below the water line causing the ship to sink.

The trireme's crew also included 20 sailors, four archers and 10 to 30 hoplites. Besides a spear, the hoplite carried a short cut-and-thrust sword and a round shield carried on his left arm. He wore greaves and a bronze helmet. He also carried a cuirass. The total weight of his armor was 70 pounds. {6-6} For the upcoming battle, the Greek triremes boarded a greater than usual number of hoplites. The fighting capabilities of the hoplites on land would now be tested on the decks of ships.

Because of their engineering capabilities, the Persian Army marched north across the Hellespont, on a bridge of boats; through Thrace and then south through Macedonia. From there, they marched south toward Athens. Simultaneously, the great army was shadowed by the Persian

Fleet, which supplied food and supplies for the marching army. The Persian Army relied upon bowmen in their infantry and also cavalry. They also used chariots to terrorize the enemy. In the mountains of Southern Greece, however, horses were not effective.

The Persian Navy utilized triremes, like the Greeks, for warships. The Persian trireme was 100 feet long and narrow in the beam. {6-7} According to the Greek historian, Herodotus, the Persian fleet contained twelve hundred vessels. {6-8} The greatest difference between the two fleets was that the Persian oarsmen were slaves while the Greek oarsmen were free men who were trained oarsmen and were depended upon to fight in battle.

The Greeks realized that to defeat the Persian Army they must first defeat the Persian Navy. Without Persian supply ships, the Persian Army would weaken. Sparta reluctantly agreed with this strategy. The next part of the strategy was the site to fight the naval battle. The Spartan general, Eurybiades, wanted to fight in the open sea. The Athenian commander, Themistocles, believed a narrow channel would favor the Greeks. He reasoned that the greater number of Persian ships would not count for much in a narrow channel. The outnumbered Greeks would have a better opportunity to win. Themistocles got his way and immediately ordered the evacuation of Athens. The Athenians were ferried from Attica to the island of Salamis. This was a wise move, since the Persians soon occupied the Acropolis. Athens was burned.

Xerxes and his generals exercised excellent strategic design, diplomacy and administrative details in their preparation for the invasion of Greece. To prevent the strong Greek colonies in Sicily from joining in the upcoming battle, Xerxes made a treaty with Carthage. The Carthaginians were to attack Sicily when the Persians attacked Greece. {6-9} Xerxes also ordered the Phoenicians, a well-known seafaring people who were allied with the Persians, to lead the attacking fleet. Greece faced a formidable enemy.

Xerxes believed his superior numbers could overwhelm the smaller Greek force in the channel between Salamis and Attica. The remnants of the Greek naval force would then be forced into the wide-open Bay of Eleusis. Here the smaller Greek force would then be destroyed by the Persian Navy, attacking from all sides. The evening before the battle, he ordered the Egyptian fleet to sail around the Island of Salamis to block the escape of the retreating Greek forces.

So confident was Xerxes of winning the upcoming naval battle that he set up a magnificent throne on a hill in Attica overlooking the channel between Salamis and Attica. He was guarded by 10,000 immortals, his personal bodyguard.

On the morning of the battle, the Persian fleet moved, several rows deep, into the channel. At one point, the channel narrowed, which caused the Persian ships to become entangled and confused. At that moment, the Greeks attacked. Superior numbers counted for nothing. The Greek ships grappled the Persian ships and a land battle ensued upon the ship's decks. The Greek hoplites were masters at close quarter fighting. The Persian archers, though, were trained to fight the enemy at a distance by shooting arrows and darts to confuse and disorganize the enemy. Once disorganized the Persians would then attack individual enemy soldiers by two or more Persians.

A Persian witness to the battle wrote: "At first the Persian line withstood the attack, but quickly the channel was crowded with our ships, and they could not aid each other. Soon their armored prows were crashing into friendly hulls and shearing off the banks of oars, while the Greek ships skillfully circled round them and attacked from all sides." {6-10}.

The battle was over in about seven hours. {6-11} Instead of witnessing a great naval victory, Xerxes witnessed a terrible Persian disaster. He witnessed his ships sinking and his sailors and soldiers screaming in death. The Persians lost 200 ships while the Greeks lost 40.

Some years after the battle, Lord Byron wrote: {6-12)

A king sat on the rocky brow
Which looks o'er sea-born Salamis;
And ships, by thousands, lay below,
And men in nations; –all were his!
He counted them at break of day–
An when the sun set where were they?

Xerxes then ordered a retreat. With half his army and most of his remaining ships, he crossed the Hellespont and the safety of Anatolia. He left about 100,000 men in Greece under the command of General Mardonius. {6-13} This Persian force secured most of Northern Greece for Persia.

About a year after the naval battle of Salamis, General Mardonius ordered the Persian Army to march south. The Persians captured Athens again, but then retreated upon learning of a Greek Army marching to oppose them. A Greek Army of about 80,000 men, composed mostly of Athenians and Spartans plus a lesser number of other Greek allies, were under the command of Spartan King Pausanias. The Greeks pursued the Persians cautiously. {6-14} The Persians retreated to a river just south of Thebes, near the town of Plataea. Both armies faced each other for about eight days without taking offensive action. The Persians then saw an opportunity. They sent their cavalry on a raid behind the Greek positions. They intercepted supply trains coming from Athens and polluted springs from which the Greeks obtained water.

The Greeks then believed that it would be expedient to fall back to new positions at the base of the mountains. This move would ensure their getting supplies and good water. The Greeks made this move during the cover of night. During the withdrawal, however, some of the Greek units lost their way in the darkness. When morning came, the Persians discovered the Greeks were divided into three uncoordinated units. The Persians grasped the opportunity to crush the Greeks in detail and immediately ordered a cavalry attack. The attack fell mainly on the Spartan's positions. After completion of the cavalry attack, the Persians believed the Spartans were disorganized and ordered an infantry assault to finish the Spartans in a close quarter battle.

This order was a Persian miscalculation. They were not aware of the superior training and discipline mastered by the Spartans. The Spartans counterattacked and inflicted terrible loses on the Persians. The battle ended after 50,000 Persians were killed. The Greek losses were about 1,300.

The Greek victories at Salamis and Plataea were decisive. Greece was freed of Persian domination, but only as long as Greece maintained its armed forces. The Persian Empire remained the dominate power in Asia.

The greatest victory, though, was freeing Greek thought. Greece, at the time, was the only country with liberty, freedom and openness to accept new thoughts. Without these victories, Greece might never have produced Sophocles, Herodotus, Pythagoras, Socrates, Plato or Aristotle who made notable contributors to Western Civilization. English Philosopher, John Stuart Mill, wrote of Greece, "the indispensable first steps, which are the foundation of all the rest." It should be noted that the Constitution of the United States was shaped in accordance with classical Greek models. {6-15}

If Persia won the war, not only Greece but also all Europe would forever fall in an abyss of dictatorships, totalitarianism, despotism and tyranny. Examine the nations in Asia today. Tragically, only the nations in Western Europe and North America have respect for the dignity of the individual.

More than a century after the Battle of Salamis, Greece produced Alexander the Great. He spread Greek thought to Europe, Asia and Africa. He is credited with carrying the elements of Western Civilization throughout the known world. His victories also marked the ascendancy of Europe over Asia.

Probably unawares, the United States occupies a position in history similar to Greece in 480 B.C. The United States is the last bastion of hope in the Free World. In the 20th Century, the United States relied on European democracies, such as Britain and France, to hold the line against tyrants. Now, Britain and France are exhausted from fighting in two World Wars. They have lost their empires. The United States, like Greece in 480 B. C, is democracy's first and last line of defense. Abraham Lincoln said, "America is the last best hope of man on earth." {6-16} At the end of World War II, British Historian Arthur Herman concluded, "With their mighty army, navy, and air force, the Americans would have to do the heavy lifting from now on." {6-17}

In the darkest days of World War II, France had fallen and the British Army was just rescued from the beaches of Dunkirk, France. In September 1939, Hitler's Germany invaded Poland. Britain and France then declared war on Germany. After the German Army overran Poland, it turned about and invaded France. France fell after a few weeks and the British Expeditionary Force in France was barely able to escape annihilation.

British Prime Minister Winston Churchill then delivered a speech that defined the British position. The speech was delivered before the House of Commons on June 18, 1940. Part of the speech is as follows: "What General Weygand called the Battle of France is over. The Battle of Britain is about to begin. On this battle depends the survival of Christian civilization. Upon it depends our own British life and long continuity of our institutions and our empire. The whole fury and might of the enemy must very soon be turned upon us. Hitler knows he will have to break us in this island or lose the war. If we can stand up to him all Europe may be freed and the life of the world may move forward into broad sunlit uplands; but if we fail, the whole world, including the

United States and all that we have known and cared for, will sink into the abyss of a new dark age made more sinister and perhaps more prolonged by the lights of a perverted science. Let us therefore brace ourselves to our duty and so bear ourselves that if the British Commonwealth and Empire last for a thousand years, men will still say 'This was their finest hour.'" {6-18}

At the time, Churchill knew the United States would not permit the Western Democracies to be trampled under. Later, he was to say, "You can always rely on America to do the right thing once it has exhausted the alternatives." {6-19}

Early in the life of the United States, "Doing the right thing" became an American characteristic. In 1801 to 1805, the United States became entangled with the Barbary Pirates of North Africa. Pirates from satellite states of Ottoman Turkey: Algiers, Tripoli and Tunis plus independent Morocco raided merchant chips in the Mediterranean Sea and the nearby Atlantic Ocean. {6-20} These countries demanded a tribute for the protection of merchant ships flying the flags of other countries. The Europeans were at war with Napoleon at the time and paid the tribute and received the promised protection.

The United States took a different tack. The United States refused to pay. Thereupon, Tripoli declared war on the United States. President Thomas Jefferson sent a punitive expedition to North Africa. The United States just adopted its Constitution in 1787. This was not the time to become engaged in a foreign war. The American people though gave President Jefferson their wholehearted support. Their battle cry was, "Millions for defense, but not one cent for tribute." {6-21}

America, early in its life, was a champion of doing the right thing. People who have lived a life of freedom and liberty in a democracy will not willingly compromise with tyrants. The Greeks in 480 BC lit the light of freedom. The Greeks knew that their freedom was worth the struggle even though the odds of success appeared unsurmountable. Their victory over the Persians saved Europe from tyranny and preserved democracy; so that it could grow and support a basis for free and independent reasoning.

The underlying purpose of NATO is expressed in Article 2 of the preamble of the Treaty. "Its goal is to preserve and improve the basic values of the civilization of Western Man, *homo Atlanticaus*." . . . .

The United States cannot rest on its past victories. British Historian, Paul Johnson, noted, "One of the great lessons of history is that no civilization can be taken for granted. Its permanency can never be assured. There is always a dark age waiting for you around the corner if you play your cards badly and you make sufficient mistakes." {6-22}.There will not be a best of seven series. There will be only one opportunity to win or lose.

General Douglas MacArthur said, "In war, there is no substitute for victory." {6-23} Liberty and freedom for Western Man should be the goal of American resolve.

CHAPTER 7

THE PERILOUS SEAS

THE ATLANTIC AND Pacific Oceans are marvelous defensive barriers for the United States. They are also terrible barriers for offensive operations. The two oceans are two-edged swords: excellent defenses but are a deterrent to offensive operations. In order to engage an enemy in the Eastern Hemisphere, the United States must circumvent one or perhaps both oceans.

Although the British Navy was probably the strongest in the world during World War I, it was still unable to neutralize the German submarine menace. In 1915, one million tons of merchant shipping bound for Britain were sunk. {7-1} In 1916, 300,000 tons per month of ships bound for Britain were sunk. {7-2} Between February and April 1917, 875,000 tons per month of merchant shipping were sunk. {7-3} By July 1917, Britain anticipated running out of food.

The German submariners were on their own when they put out to sea. There were no capital ships to support them if a strong enemy force had engaged them. Except German Southwest Africa, there were no foreign bases available for refueling etc.

In World War II, German submarines achieved similar results. During the first three months of 1943, German submarines sunk 108 merchant ships bound for Britain. {7-4} British food supply was reduced to no more than three more months.

Since World War II, submarines have undergone massive improvements. By comparison, World War II submarines were built with comparative Stone Age technology. They had a depth limit of 400 feet; {7-1} they had to surface to communicate and charge their batteries. Above all, the sailors aboard the submarines could not endure the stressful environment for more than a few months at sea. {7-5}

Submariners were required to live in compact quarters while enduring an odor of diesel fumes and urine. To mitigate their environment, submarine crews had to return to a land base to regain their humanity. After a time, they would be ready to go to sea again.

Today's nuclear submarines are a far cry from the World War II submarines. Their only similarity is that they are both called submarines. The necular submarines are spacious and provide an excellent living environment. Men can endure living on a nuclear submarine for an extended stay. There is no need to surface to charge batteries or introduce fresh air into the submarine.

One of the weaknesses of the World War II submarine was radio communication. To communicate, the submarine had to surface or remain submerged but stay close to the surface; so that an antenna could be projected above the water level. It would seem that a small antenna exposed in the open ocean would go undetected. Spotters with advanced detection equipment located high on enemy ships were specifically trained to recognize submarine antennas. Once detected, a submarine's usefulness was neutralized in a particular area. The submarine may not be sunk or damaged, but it alerts the enemy that there are hostile submarines in the area. The submarine's main strength lies in its ability to remain undetected.

Although a nuclear submarine is superior to a World War II submarine in every way, it is still wanting in radio communications. Without communications a military unit becomes a disorganized mob. New technology, however, has overcome the radio communications defect. The new technology permits the submarine to remain submerged while communicating. {7-6} This technology is employed by ejecting a buoy through the submarines trash chute. Once ejected into the water, the buoy will hover at a predetermined depth. The submarine moves away from the buoy, and after short time, the buoy will surface and send messages to the command and control center. Once a communications link is established with the command and control center, the buoy will lower an antenna deep into the water. Messages are then sent through a transducer that translates the messages into acoustic energy and then sends a pulse out into the water that encompasses an area more than 50 nautical square miles.

One of the challenges to this communications system was different thermal layers in the ocean that caused different consistencies. This defect was overcome by sending multiple signals over the transmitter.

More new technologies are constantly improving submarines. There is good reason for submariners to say there are just two kinds of ships: submarines and targets.

In addition to submarines, merchant ships must contend with underwater mines. Innocent looking fishing vessels and merchant ships can lay mines. Submarines can also lay mines. Generally, a submarine can carry two mines in place of each torpedo. {7-7}.

A naval mine weighs between 1,000 and 2,000 pounds. There are several mine designs, which makes them difficult to detect and clear. There are free-floating mines, moored mines, mobile mines, captor mines, remote-controlled mines, contact mines, magnetic-influence mines, acoustic mines, and pressure mines. Mines may also be equipped with microcomputers that are designed to select a type of target.

During World War II, German mines closed eight American ports for 40 days. The port of Charleston, South Carolina was closed for 16 days. The German submarine mine laying campaign between 1942 and 1944 laid 317 mines and sank or damaged 11 ships. This resulted in a ratio of 29 mines per ship sunk {7-8}. Mines have the advantage of relatively low cost and of tying-up enemy time and resources while the mines are cleared.

During World War II in the Pacific Theater, American submarines laid 658 mines, which sunk or damaged 54 ships. This was a ratio of one ship per 12 mines. American mines also closed the port on the Palau atoll. It was never opened again. American aircraft also laid mines. During a 10 week period in 1945, 12,000 mines were delivered by air. These mines struck or damaged 1,100 Japanese ships or 18 mines for each ship sunk or damaged.

The use of naval mines is a relatively inexpensive way to conduct naval war. However, the addition of surface ships, submarines and aircraft forces the enemy to defend against several modes of attack. During World War II, German submarines were winning the naval war in the Atlantic until the Allies began using aircraft to search and destroy German submarines. The German Air Force did not have the resources to interdict the Allied air offensive over the Atlantic. The German Air Force was pushed to it limits by defending against Allied air raids over Europe and offensive missions in Russia. Thus, the German submarine effort in the Atlantic was defeated by a combination of Allied surface ships and aircraft.

Some military analysts contend that a naval war with Russia would be short lived as Russian ships would be forced to negotiate narrow passages or choke points. The Russian Northern Fleet must pass over Norway's North Cape before reaching the Atlantic. After passing over the North Cape, the Russian fleet would then have to pass over SOSUS (Sound Surveillance System), a series of sensors lying on the ocean floor between Britain, Iceland and Greenland. This system named CAESAR, LISTENS TO EVERYTHING CROSSING OVER IT up to a distance of 180 km (113 miles) {7-9} Information obtained from the sensors is passed on to data processing centers and then to naval commanders that recommend appropriate action.

The Russian Baltic Fleet must first pass through the Kattegat and then over the SOSUS system before entering the Atlantic. The Black Sea Fleet must pass through the Dardanelles before reaching the Mediterranean Sea and then through the Strait of Gibraltar before reaching the Atlantic. The Pacific Fleet located at Vladivostok must pass through the Korea Strait before entering the Pacific. {7-10

This concept, however, was based upon the NATO strategy during the Cold War. Since then, great technical improvements have been made, especially with submarines. Nuclear submarines are no longer required to traverse choke points. They have the capability of staying submerged indefinitely. Russia borders the Arctic Ocean, which is icebound most of the year. A Russian nuclear submarine could simply go under the Arctic ice and then into waters not controlled by NATO.

An excellent Russian submarine base lies in waters that have easy access to the Pacific Ocean. This base, Sovetskaya Gavan, is some 700 miles north of the big Russian naval base at Vladlvostok. The latter base is located in the Sea of Japan and on the wrong side of the Japanese island chain. On the other hand, the port of Sovetskaya Gavan, which is supplied by the Trans-Siberian Railroad, lies west of Sakhalin Island. Sakhalin affords protection from an enemy attacking from the east and becomes, therefore, a protected base.

From its base at Sovetskaya Gavan, Russian submarines could travel north to the Sea of Oskhotsk and then turn south through the Russian owned Kuril Islands. From the Kuril Islands, the Russian submarines would then be in the open Pacific Ocean and all other oceans of the world. The Russian submarine fleet would become Russia's offensive naval arm.

The Russian surface fleet would probably be used to defend its home ports and waters. The Russian surface navy occupies a similar position as the German surface navy in World War II. The German Navy was somewhat landlocked, and its warships numbered far less than the number of ships in the British Navy.

The strategy of the German surface navy was the destruction of British merchant ships. {7-11} Although the German warships had big guns and armor protection to engage British warships, they did not have the numbers for an all-out engagement with the British Navy.

In 1939, German warship Graf Spee raided British merchant ships in the South Atlantic Ocean. After capturing and sinking 11 merchant ships, the Graf Spee was discovered by three British naval ships off Argentina. The German and British ships immediately engaged in battle. After about two hours of battle, the British and German vessels were put out of action. The Graf Spee took refuge in Montevideo for repairs. {7-12} The Uruguayan government would permit the Graf Spee only 72 hours of sanctuary. By that time, more British warships arrived on the scene. The Graf Spee sailed out of Montevideo and was scuttled.

Other German surface raiders met a similar fate. Probably the most effective German surface ship was the battleship Tirpitz, the sister ship of the Bismarck Battleship, {7-13}. The Tirpitz was anchored in Norway and represented a threat in being. It held many British warships in port and ready to attack the Tirpitz if it ventured out to sea. The held British ships could have been better used to escort merchant chips in the Atlantic. The Tirpitz, however, did participate in a raid on Spitsbergen and the allied shipping run to Murmansk.

From the lessons learned from World War II, the Russian naval strategy would probably use its nuclear submarine fleet for offensive action and its surface fleet for defensive measures. Its nuclear submarine fleet could far outweigh any offensive action possessed by its surface fleet. The nuclear submarine is the optimum of warships in a future war. During World War I, the battleship was queen of the sea. In World War II, that title belonged to the aircraft carrier, and in a future war, the nuclear submarine will carry the title.

To transport war material to the Eastern Hemisphere, the United States' merchant vessels will be forced to cross the huge Atlantic and Pacific Oceans. The size of these oceans provides an opportunity for the enemy to make several attacks on merchant ships in the crossing. America's past experience in war was that it delivered about 95 percent of its war material in surface ships. The possibility of supplying sufficient war materials by ship in today's environment to the Eastern Hemisphere is remote. Today's surface warships and merchant ships have not changed significantly since World War II. Submarines and sea mines, though, have vastly improved.

To achieve favorable results, the United States must seek an alternative to seaborne transport. The obvious choice is airlift. The United States successfully supplied Israel by air during the Yom Kippur War in 1973. At the time, the Israeli Armed Forces consisted of about 300,000 men, {7-14} and combat operations ceased after about two weeks. A major war with China or Russia would require an American armed force of about three million men with war operations continuing for about a year. When Germany launched an attack on the Soviet Union in 1941, its attacking force numbered about three million men. {7-15} The war continued for four years.

At present the United States Air Force is using three airlift aircraft: the C-5, C-17 and C-130. These are excellent airlift aircraft, but the United States does not have an adequate number of them. In 2008, the fleet was at "the ragged edge of the minimum" for the job. {7-24} Compounding the inadequacy of airlift is the fact that 300 C-17 aircraft are required to equal the capacity of one standard large medium speed roll-on/roll-off sea cargo vessel. A successful airlift must equal the capacity of sea transport vessels. A NATO army division would require 2,240 tons of supplies per day. A 90-day level of supplies for 24 NATO divisions would require 4.9 million tons of supplies for wartime operations. {7-16}

A capable solution to the transport problem would involve the use of zeppelin airships. Germany used zeppelins in World War I. After the war, the United States and Britain experimented with zeppelins. After several accidents and the crash of the Hindenburg zeppelin in 1937, the interest in military zeppelins declined. The principal defect of the Hindenburg zeppelin was its use of hydrogen gas for lift. Hydrogen is a very flammable gas. Later airship designs use Helium gas for lift. Helium is an inert gas that can be used as a fire extinguisher. Incidentally the Hindenburg's design was a forerunner of the future.

Now, a new interest in zeppelins has returned. {7-17} Several airship designs that are operational are the Cargo Lifter in Germany {7-18} and the Megalifter {7-19} in the United States. There are several other designs, but only two are mentioned here.

The German Cargo Lifter can carry 160 tons at 50 miles per hour.

The Megalifter can carry 200 tons and travel at a speed of 175 knots. An ocean going military cargo vessel can carry 24,000 tons at an average speed of 18 knots. {7-20} Thus, the cargo vessel holds more than 100 times the Megalifter, but the Megalifter is about 10 times faster.

The Meglifter's lift capacity is twice the lift of a C-5 aircraft. A distinguishing characteristic of the Megalifter is its airplane wing. The wing offers stability and reduces rolling and yawing. Also, the cockpit of the Megalifter is like the inside of a C-5 aircraft and has four jet engines.

Some of the heavy equipment required for combat operations are the Abrams tank which weighs 70 tons and the Crusader artillery piece which weighs 40 tons. The Pentagon is considering canceling the Crusader, as it is deemed too heavy to transport. {7-21} Nevertheless, the Army requires heavy equipment. Only a C-5 and a C-17 aircraft can carry an Abrams tank and only one tank per plane. {7-22}.

If the United States procured 100 Megalifter dirigibles, it could deliver 20,000 tons of supplies in one day across the Atlantic or Pacific Oceans. After a few weeks, the Megalifter loads could equal the load of a sea going vessel. The sea vessel, though, would also face multiple dangers of being sunk.

To be successful, the dirigibles must have an advanced staging base. If the war area is in the western part of the Eastern Hemisphere, a good staging base would be the Azores. The Azores were successfully used as an advanced staging base in the 1973 Yom Kippur War. The dirigibles must be looked upon as sea-going ships. They are big, bulky and not maneuverable. Thus, they cannot be used to fly military equipment to the battle area.

Once the dirigibles arrive at the staging base, they should be unloaded and their loads transferred to C-5 and C-17 aircraft. The C-5 and C-17 aircraft could then fly the equipment and supplies to the battle area as was done by the Israelis during the Yom Kippur War. During the Yom Kippur War, the Israelis required runways to land the aircraft and then unload them. A future war may not require the need of runways to unload aircraft. A new capability, the JPADS or Joint Precision Air Drop System has been developed. In tests, a 2,000 pound pallet was parachuted from an aircraft to within a few feet of designated coordinates of a drop zone. The JPADS system used a GPS aided navigation system similar to the one used on "smart" bombs. {7-23}

One advantage attributed to dirigibles is low fuel consumption.

Except for the Megalifter, many dirigibles are powered by diesel engines. The lift of all dirigibles is provided by helium gas. An airplane, on the other hand, obtains its thrust and lift from its engines. Therefore, its fuel consumption is far greater than a dirigible.

When flying over the oceans, the dirigibles must be escorted by fighter aircraft and unmanned drone aircraft. The high-flying unmanned drones will provide a warning of upcoming dangers. The dirigibles will probably fly low to minimize the detection on an enemy's radar screen.

CHAPTER 8

MILITARY POWER

SOME ANALYSTS CONTEND that national power and military power are one and the same. A political analyst, Dr. Clifford German, advised that the factors in national power included: land area, population, the national economy and military power. {8-1} There might be some disagreement on the amount of weight that should be placed on each factor. Indeed, three centuries earlier, Francis Bacon, the English statesman, concluded: "There is not anything amongst civil affairs more subject to error than the right evaluation and true judgment concerning the power and forces of a state."

Nevertheless, military power and national power are distinct entities, although military power is a component of national power. Military power consists of training, tactics, weapons, and morale. {8-2} General Eisenhower suggested that the components of military power are a *product* and not a sum. Thus, if morale went to zero so does military power.

Morale is a curious element in the human psychic. It cannot be accurately defined and cannot be measured. In the business world morale is an unknown quantity. Employees work for wages, and they are looked upon as equipment parts that are interchangeable. Managers look upon morale as having no monetary value, and therefore, worthless. In a typical well-managed business, the employees are constantly competing with one another to curry favor from a supervisor. As a result morale is low and most often does not exist, but the bottom line is increased profit.

By contrast, a military organization is a team or unit in which every member is supportive. In combat, every member of the team unit trusts his very life on every other team member. Trust is a great part of morale, which is developed over time: through unit training and in the use of weapons. Over time, of about some six weeks, each member of the unit learns to trust each member of the unit. To reinforce trust, members of a unit should gather together for off duty social activities.

A few years before the United States entered World War II, Fort Sam Houston, Texas housed the Second Infantry Division and associated artillery. Soldiers in the infantry and artillery wore the same uniform. The only distinguishing item between the two branches of service was the barely perceptible braid worn on the soldiers' hats. Artillery men wore a red braid while infantrymen wore a blue braid.

After duty hours, many of the soldiers visited the bars near the fort. In time, blue braids and red braids became territorial. Blue braids or red braids would permit only braids of the same color to drink at a bar. Consequently, men wearing one color braid attempted to force the men wearing another color braid from the bar. There was nothing vicious, only a playful incidental activity. Though, a casual observer would only see brawling soldiers. Unknowingly, the soldiers developed a sense of trust and that they were part of something larger than themselves.

During World War I, a stalemate developed on the Western Front. A series of trenches were dug from Switzerland to the English Channel. The opposing armies attempted breakthroughs, but all failed. Finally a German officer, Captain Rohr, proposed forming elite infantry units that would break through and force a gap in the enemy trenches that would then permit the regular infantry to follow the elite unit and exploit the break through.

The elite infantry units, *stosstruppen*, were composed of men in superb physical condition and commanded by young lieutenants or captains. One *stosstruppen* commander related about a fellow commander, "Markmann knew precisely how he stood with his men. To them he was not their commanding officer; he was their Leader! And they were his Comrades! They trusted him blindly and would have followed him into hell itself if it were necessary." {8-3}

Markmann's unit represented the ultimate in trust, leadership, group cohesion and esprit de corps. None of these qualities can be measured or defined: but, nonetheless, they are essential to winning battles and ultimately winning wars. Military units in general should strive to duplicate Markmann's unit. Moreover, without the stress of combat, this goal may be difficult to achieve.

In World War I, American soldiers were called dough boys. This name was probably the result of America's entry in the war three years after the war began. American soldiers were like fresh dough ready to be put in the oven.

In World War II, American soldiers called themselves GIs, which is an abbreviation for government issue. Not all American soldiers were entitled to the term GI. Army Air Force personnel were not awarded the term. Air Force personnel sustained heavy casualties in combat, but at the end of a mission, they received a warm meal and slept in a soft bed. On the other hand, a GI slept in a muddy fox hole and occasionally received a hot meal.

In the Viet Nam War, the American Pentagon seemed to prefer the term: government issue. The Secretary of Defense during the Viet Nam War, Robert McNamara, used computer efficiencies, system analysis and linear logic. If a unit in Viet Nam requested two riflemen and three trucks, the Pentagon would ship two riflemen and three trucks to the unit. Equipment and personnel were interchangeable, disposable parts. Personnel were shipped in like temporary office workers. Admiral Grace Hopper noted: "Things are managed while people are led."

America's involvement in the Viet Nam War was probably the most inept war ever conducted by the United States. Sending soldiers individually to a war zone instead of in cohesive units confused the new soldiers, as they were not part of the established unit. Trust in the new unit was absent for the new men and as well for the unit's experienced veteran's trust in the new men. All of the soldiers were not confident in the other soldier's resolve. Would he stand and fight or flee?

From a corporate executive perspective, America's involvement in the Viet Nam War was undoubtedly an efficient well-managed war. The Secretary of Defense, Robert McNamara, was probably a successful industrial manager, but management techniques are the most flawed for military operations. The military services, however, are subject to civilian control. The President of the United States is the commander in chief of the Armed Forces. The Armed Forces, though, can best perform their duties when they are not micro- managed. At one time during the Viet Nam War, the President of the United States, Lyndon Johnson boasted, "They can't even bomb an outhouse without my approval" {8-5} A military commander's training and experience can best determine targets; so that victory can be achieved. If a civilian manager overrides the views of a military commander, the objective may not be achieved, and further, the end result may create higher casualties. Above all, morale, which is essential to military operations, is ignored.

. . . .

On December 7, 1941, the United States abruptly entered World War II. Japan's naval aircraft attacked America's Pacific Fleet anchored at Pearl Harbor, Hawaii. Most of the American battleships were sunk or badly damaged in the raid. Fortuitously, the aircraft carriers were away on patrol when the raid occurred. The American Pacific Fleet, however, was neutralized. In order to have an effective combat force, the navy as well as all combat forces, must have redundancy. Battleships protect aircraft carriers from enemy surface ships, and planes on aircraft carriers protect battleships from enemy aircraft.

The United States anticipated a possible war with Japan. Japan became a recognized military power after it defeated the Russians in the Russo-Japanese War in 1904-1905. In a possible war with Japan, American military commanders believed that the Philippines would receive the initial assault by the Japanese military. Consequently, a strong defense of the Luzon peninsula in northern Philippine Islands was predicated. This defense would then be supported by a strong counterattack by the U.S. Pacific Fleet. {8-6} The destruction of the Pacific Fleet dashed the American military plan. The remaining striking power of the Pacific fleet consisted of three aircraft carriers.

With the American Pacific Fleet neutralized, there was no other force in the Pacific to challenge the Japanese southward advance. Britain needed all its forces to defend against German submarines in the Atlantic. In anticipation of a Japanese attack, Britain did dispatch two capital ships to Singapore: *The Prince of Wales and The Repulse*. These two ships were quickly attacked and sunk by Japanese aircraft soon after the Pearl Harbor attack.

France and the Netherlands held colonies in Southeast Asia, but their armed forces in Asia were of no consequence, since their governments were knocked out of the war by the German Army operating in Europe. The American people, though, were up in arms. Japan needed to be punished for its treachery. Japan was the obvious enemy of the United States.

Be that as it may, Germany, however, declared war on the United States on December 11, 1941. America was then also at war with Germany. The Prime Minister of Britain, Winston Churchill, persuaded the American president, Franklin Roosevelt, to adopt a "Europe first strategy." {8-7}. This strategy, called War Plan 5, was adopted in June

1941, prior to the Japanese attack on Pearl Harbor. A defensive strategy was then allotted to the Philippines and the rest of Asia. On Christmas Day, 1941, Prime Minister Winston Churchill again visited President Franklin Roosevelt at the White House to sustain America's adoption of War Plan 5. {8-8}

The commander of the American armed forces in the Philippines, General Douglas MacArthur, was not immediately aware of War Plan 5. Consequently, he prepared the Philippine defense on the belief that a relief force was on its way. On December 30, 1941, President Roosevelt dispatched the following message: {8-9}

> NEWS OF YOUR GALLANT STRUGGLE AGAINST THE JAPANESE AGGRESSORS HAS ELICITED THE PROFOUND ADMIRATION OF EVERY AMERICAN CITIZEN. I GIVE TO THE PEOPLE OF THE PHILIPPINES MY SOLEMN PLEDGE THAT THEIR FREEDOM WILL BE REDEEMED AND THEIR INDEPENDENCE ESTABLISHED AND PROTECTED. THE ENTIRE RESOURCES IN MEN AND MATERIALS OF THE UNITED STATES STANDS BEHIND THIS PLEDGE.

With this news, the Philippine defenders were euphoric. They were not forgotten. Their morale was lifted. In their excitement, however, they failed to hear when the help would arrive.

On January 15, 1942, the commander of the U.S. Army, George C. Marshall, issued the following communiqué: {8-10}

> A STREAM OF FOUR-ENGINE BOMBERS, PREVIOUSLY DELAYED BY FOUL WEATHER, IS EN ROUTE . . . ANOTHER STREAM OF SIMILAR BOMBERS STARTED TODAY FROM HAWAII STAGING AT A NEW ISLAND FIELDS. TWO GROUPS OF POWERFUL MEDIUM BOMBERS OF LONG RANGE AND HEAVY BOMB LOAD CAPACITY LEAVE NEXT WEEK. PURSUIT PLANES ARE COMING ON EVERY SHIP WE CAN USE . . . EVERY DAY OF TIME YOU GAIN IS VITAL TO THE CONCENTRATION OF THE OVERWHELMING POWER NECESSARY TO OUR PURPOSE

Most American people were not aware of communiqués from Washington, D.C. They knew what they read in their local newspapers.

The Japanese forces were moving south and east at a rapid pace. The United States was doing nothing to impede the Japanese. Army Air Force General Curtis E. LeMay noted, "Our entire nation howled like a pack of wolves for an attack on the Japanese homeland."{8-11} Churchill, though, had convinced Roosevelt that the German submarine menace was a greater danger. {8-12}.

Hong Kong fell on December 25, 1941. Malaya and Singapore fell on February 15. 1942. (The big guns at Singapore were sited out to sea for a naval attack and could not be turned to face the land side. The Japanese Army attacked from the land {8-13}.) The Dutch East Indies, the Solomon Islands, and most of New Guinea were in Japanese control by March 1942. Thus, the American and Filipino troops in the Philippines were cut off from any possible assistance. Bataan fell on April 9, 1942. Corregidor, the last bastion in the Philippines, surrendered to the Japanese on May 6, 1942.

War correspondent Frank Hewlett wrote of the defenders of the Philippines: {8-14}

We are the battling bastards of Bataan
No mamma, no pappa, no Uncle Sam
No aunts, no uncles, no nephews, no nieces
No rifles, no guns or artillery pieces
And nobody gives a damn!

Thus, the morale of the American people became extremely low. Australia could be next to fall to Japan. How could America win the war after suffering so many defeats? President Roosevelt apparently saw something else. He ordered his military commanders to draw-up a plan to bomb the Japanese home islands. This seemed an impossible task. The nearest American base to the Japanese home islands, which had not been overrun by Japanese forces, was Midway Island in the Central Pacific. Midway, though, could not be used, since it was about 3500 miles from Japan. American commanders contended that the bombers would best be flown from a base no further than about 500 miles from Japan. An aircraft carrier was such a base. ``

President Roosevelt wished to attack Japan from East Chinese bases, {8-15} but he deferred to the judgment of the military commanders. The commanders concluded that B-25 bombers flown from the deck of the *Hornet* could do the job. On the return mission, however, the B-25 bombers could not land on the *Hornet*. After the bomb runs over Japan, the bombers would fly on to friendly areas in China. {8-16}

Thus, land-based B-25 Mitchell bombers would fly from the deck of an aircraft carrier. Such a feat had never been done before. The deck of an aircraft carrier was designed to accommodate relatively small single engine aircraft. The Navy aircraft required a shorter take off distance; an Army bomber required a much longer take off distance.

Once the naval requirements were satisfied, it was then time for the Army airmen to adhere to these requirements. In January 1942, Army Air Force General Henry H. Arnold asked, "Jim (Doolittle), what airplane have we got that will get off in 500 feet with a 2,000 pound bomb load and fly 2,000 miles." {8-17}

On March 7, 1942, about 140 pilots and their crews assembled before Colonel Jimmy Doolittle at Eglin Air Force Base, Florida. All of the airmen were volunteers for an unknown dangerous mission. Doolittle immediately addressed the men: "If you men have any idea that this isn't the most dangerous mission you've been on, don't even start this training period. You can drop out now. There isn't much sense wasting time and money training men who aren't going through with this thing. It's perfectly all right for any of you to drop out." (8-18) None dropped out. The air crews were sworn to secrecy.

To simulate a take-off from a carrier's deck, air crews marked-off the distance on a concrete runway that was the same as the distance on an aircraft carrier's flight deck. All of the air crews successfully completed the training. However, only 110 of the original 140 crewmen were selected for the mission. Thus, 30 crewmen were trained replacements.

Twenty-two B-25s of Doolittle's mission were then ordered to fly to the Alameda Naval Air Station, California. Here, the planes were loaded onto the aircraft carrier, *Hornet*. Once the loading began, the pilots realized that the carrier's deck was becoming too short for a successful take off. The flight decks became too short when all 22 planes were loaded on the *Hornet's* deck. The Doolittle Raiders were then reduced to 16 B-25s.

On April 2, 1942, the *Hornet* sailed out of San Francisco Bay. The *Hornet* was escorted by 15 ships including the aircraft carrier *Enterprise*. The naval task force steamed to an area northwest of Midway Island. On April 17, the task force was about 800 miles from Tokyo when an enemy ship was sighted. It was assumed that the enemy ship reported the sighting of the American task force. Doolittle was then faced with the dilemma of aborting the mission or launching the B-25s sooner than planned.

He decided to go, although the take off was 10 hours sooner than planned. At 8:20 a.m., Doolittle was in the first plane to depart the *Hornet's* deck. He had planned to be over Tokyo at night and the incendiary bombs dropped from his plane would light the way for the B-25 planes following him. His first bomb was dropped at 12:25 p.m. {8-19}

The last plane to take off from the *Hornet* was airborne at 9:19 a.m. The bombs from all 16 B-25s struck military targets in Japan. Afterwards, the raiders were to fly to bases in China. Although a fortuitous tail wind gave the planes an extra 250 miles distance, the planes were forced to fly a much greater distance than was planned with the allotted fuel. {8-20}

Doolittle, flying the lead plane, anticipated reaching the Chinese coast at dawn. Instead, he reached China at night. Trying to land a plane at night in an unknown area without landing lights is too great a hazard to risk. Doolittle put the plane on automatic pilot. Then he and his crew parachuted from the plane at about 9:15 p.m. and landed in a rice paddy. After flying some 2,250 miles, he reached Chuchow, China, which was about 200 miles south of Shanghai and 70 miles inland.

The other air crews suffered the same fate as Doolittle and had to abandon their planes before landing at a Chinese air strip. Most had to parachute to the ground. Three crew members died on landing, and eight more were captured by the Japanese. Of these, three were summarily executed, one died of malnutrition and four survived in a Japanese prison until the end of the war. The remaining air crews found safety in China. One plane, having engine trouble, safely flew to the Soviet Union and the crew was interred.

The Doolittle raid on Tokyo did no significant military damage, but it gave the American people a huge boost in morale Americans then believed their country was on the right course, and the war could be won. It was that intangible quality, *morale*, that made the difference. The air crews of the Doolittle raiders flew a very dangerous and nearly impossible mission that boosted the morale of the American people. The value of morale in wartime cannot be overstated.

The Doolittle Raid not only improved American morale, but also caused the decline of Japanese morale. An eyewitness to the Doolittle raid, Toshiko Matsumura, gave this account, "My people had always placed emphasis on spiritual strength and the medieval belief that Japan would never be attacked. As children we had been taught to believe what the Emperor and his advisers told us. It was a severe psychological shock to even the most ardent believer when it was announced that we had been attacked. The eventual effect was great but was not immediately evident. We finally began to realize that all we were told was not true-- that the Government had lied when it said we were invulnerable. We then started to doubt that we were also invincible." {8-21}

Doolittle and most of the B-25 bomber crews survived the raid. Doolittle was promoted to Brigadier General and awarded the Congressional Medal of Honor. {8-22} Generalissimo Chiang Kai-shek, the Chinese leader, had opposed the Doolittle raid, as the flyers would find sanctuary in China. This would surely bring down the wrath of the Japanese Army. As predicted, Japan dispatched an army corps to exact vengeance on the Chinese people who helped the Doolittle raiders. The Chinese government estimated that the Doolittle raid cost the lives of 250,000 Chinese people {8-23}. . .

In wartime, morale is the key to success not only for military personnel but also for the civil population. Anytime a military commander can improve morale he should act on it, enhance it, embellish it. The late Admiral Grace Hopper concluded that one manages things but leads people. The term management should be stricken from the military vocabulary. If any member of the armed forces is found using such a term, he should be horsewhipped or keelhauled where appropriate. (Keelhauled is a nautical method of punishment. A sailor is dropped into the water on one side of the boat and then pulled under the ship to the other side of the boat. The sailor will probably engage many barnacles while under the ship.).

During the years prior to the outbreak of World War I, France devised several war plans that would be enacted in the event of a war with Germany. The French people at the time felt humiliated by Germany. Some four decades earlier, the Germans had detached the French provinces, Alsace and Lorraine, and made them part of Germany. The French spirit, subsequently, was elan or attack. The offense and everywhere attack became the only mind set of France. The latest war plan was enacted by the French government in October 1913. It was titled Plan XVII and included eight commandments. (8-24)

The seventh commandment which was italicized by the authors read: *"Battles are beyond everything else struggles of morale. Defeat is inevitable as soon as the hope of conquering ceases to exist. Success comes not to him who has suffered the least but to him whose will is firmest and morale strongest."*

In the initial campaign of World War I, the German Army quickly advanced through Belgium and Northern France as prescribed by the Schlieffen Plan. Its objective was the envelopment of Paris. At first, the German Army was advancing on schedule. However, the German commanders, in Berlin, away from the battle zones, seemed to have lost their nerve. They transferred troops from France and sent them to oppose the Russian threat in the East. This transfer was the absolute anathema of the Schlieffen Plan. The German front in the West was weakened and France decided to establish a defense at the Marne River. The German troops sent east arrived too late to affect the ongoing battle of Tannenberg. The war in the West became a stalemate. Both armies dug opposing trenches that extended from the North Sea to the Swiss frontier.

Napoleon concluded that wars are either maneuver or attrition. The Western Front became a war of attrition. In 1916, Germany's Chief of the general Staff, General Erich von Falkenhayn, devised a plan to win the war in the West. Falkenhayn concluded that the defense held a stronger tactical advantage than the offense. Rapid firing machine guns and other modern weapons strongly favored the defense. Falkenhayn believed that if German troops captured a symbolical city, France would send waves of French troops to recapture the city. The defending German troops would then bleed the French army white. {8-25}

Falkenhayn selected the fortified French city of Verdun to accomplish his plan. Verdun was a French national symbol of resistance. In the past, it had resisted Prussian and German attacks. The provinces of Alsace and Lorraine owe their existence to the Treaty of Verdun in 843. The fall of Verdun would be a terrible blow to French morale. The honor of France would not permit the Germans to succeed. The French general responsible for the defense of Verdun, Marshal Henri Petain, created the watchwords: *"Ils ne passeront pas!"* ("They shall not pass!") *(8-26)* Ultimately, these were the watchwords for the French Army until the end of the war.

On February 21, 1916, the German guns opened the assault on Verdun with 2,000,000 shells. The German infantry then advanced. French forces counter attacked and enlarged the battle area. Falkenhayn envisioned the battle area to be limited to the east bank of the Meuse River. Heavy guns from French artillery began firing from the west bank. The Germans were then forced to attack French positions on the west bank. Falkenhayn's plans were shattered. He also had to accede to the demands of the Eastern Front. Fifteen German divisions were transferred from Verdun to the Eastern Front to offset an ongoing major Russian offensive. The battle of Verdun ended about mid December 1916. Falkenhayn was dismissed in August 1916 and replaced with Hindenburg and Ludendorff. The exact number of casualties at the battle of Verdun is unknown. However, one source estimates the French casualties at 542,000 men and the German at 434,000 men. (8-27)

The German attack and French counter attacks at Verdun did not alter the war in the West. The commander of the French forces at Verdun, General Petain wrote, "My heart leaped as I saw our youths of twenty going into the furnace of Verdun, but how depressing it was when they returned. Their expressions seemed frozen by a vision of terror; their gait and their postures betrayed a total dejection; they sagged beneath the weight of horrifying memories." {8-28}

Nevertheless, it seemed to the new French commander that now it was France's turn to end the war in the West. In December 1916, General Robert Nivelle succeeded Marshal Joseph Jacques Cesaire Joffre as commander in chief of the French Army. Nivelle knew he had a plan to break the stalemate in the West and end the war. The war-weary *poilu*, French GI, now believed that this one more assault would bring the war to an end. Nivelle's plan would mass advancing infantry on a broad front with the support of tanks. Instead of a mass artillery barrage that preceded most attacks, the artillery would fire a swift rolling barrage just ahead of the attacking infantry. (8-30) The offense was to be carried out with "violence, brutality and rapidity."(8-31) It seemed that the whole of France knew of the Nivelle Plan. The Germans too heard of the plan and, fortunately for them, obtained a copy of the plan.

On April 5, 1917, French artillery began a rolling barrage on a 25-mile front between Rheims and Soissons. Unfortunately, the rolling barrage advanced too far ahead and too quick for the infantry to follow. When the French artillery shells passed over and then behind the reinforced German bunkers, German machine gun crews came out of their bunkers along with supporting German artillery that caught the attacking French infantry in the open. The French tanks were easily destroyed by German artillery. French casualties between April 16 and April 29 were 134,000 men. There was no French victory. The war did not end, and the stalemate continued. The war-weary French soldiers had enough and 68 of France's 112 infantry divisions mutinied.

The first indication of the mutiny was the refusal of replacement infantrymen to return to the front. (8-32) The French mutiny was not anything like the Russian mutiny in 1917. Russian soldiers shot their officers and all military order disintegrated. The French mutiny was much like workers on a strike. The soldiers had grievances, which they wanted addressed. The Nivelle offensive, along with the Verdun defense, had slaughtered and demoralized the French Army. The French government seemingly aware of the plight of the French *poilu* did not discipline the mutineers. Instead, Marshal Petain was made commander-in-chief of the French Army and assigned the task of restoring order and morale of the French troops. Petain used patience and skill and made reforms in the French military policies. Above all, he reassured the troops that France would not initiate a general offensive until tanks and American reinforcements gave the Allies unquestioned military superiority. Moreover, he restored the morale of the French Army. British Field Marshal Montgomery believed that: 'The morale of the soldier is the greatest single factor in war." {8-33}

In World War I, France mobilized 8,410,000 men for military service. She suffered 1,357,800 military dead and 4,266,000 military wounded. (8-34), or 2/3 of its mobilized force became casualties. Two decades later, France again was faced with duplicating the same sacrifice. The French government, however, anticipated a conflict with Germany. They built the Maginot Line between 1930 and 1935. The Maginot Line was a string of concrete forts spaced about three miles apart near the German frontier. The fortress line extended from the Italian and Swiss frontiers in the south to the Ardennes forest in Luxembourg in the north. The Maginot Line did not extend farther north, opposite Belgium, as this would appear that France anticipated an attack from Belgium The Ardennes Forest was a hilly, wooded area that was believed to be impenetrable. If Germany attacked France through Belgium, as it did in World War I, most of the French Army would then move against the invader in Belgium. {8-35}

The French people put their faith and trust in the Maginot Line. They would not sacrifice a whole generation of young men to a purposeless slaughter. French *elan* so pronounced in the early part of World War I was totally absent in the beginning of World War II. The Maginot Line developed into a symbol of French pacifism and order of battle, which became known as *Maginot Mentality. It affected diplomacy and military thinking.* France only thought of defending France and not offer a defense for other nations. (France did make treaty alliances with other nations such as the treaty of Locarno in 1925 whose main focus was mutual assistance. French interpretation, though, was that other nations were to assist France, but France did not intend to assist any other nation.) *Maginot Mentality*, which included the terrible casualties of World War I, destroyed French morale. It became something like a contagious disease. Fighting in a war was for a Frenchman a futile endeavor and would only bring about a person's death or permanent disability.

This spirit infected the French Army, the French people and the French political system. On September 1, 1939, Germany invaded Poland, and World War II began. A few months earlier, France and Poland had made a secret military pact. {8-36} If Germany attacked France, Poland was to attack Germany from the east. If Germany attacked Poland, France would, on the third day after mobilization, make limited attacks on Germany. After the 15th day, France would attack with a full-scale offensive.

After declaring war on Germany, Britain and France, however, took no action against Germany. They were supposedly mobilizing. In France the war was called, "*drole de guerre,*" in Britain the "twilight war," in Germany the "Sitzkrieg," and in America the "phony war." The paralysis was believed to be a fear of aerial bombardment. Britain's Committee of Imperial Defense estimated that the initial bombardment would last 60 days and kill 600,000 and maim more than one million people. {8-37}

Poland fell on October 5, 1939. Britain and France knew that now the German Army would turn about and march west. First, however, German forces marched into Denmark and Norway. Denmark fell on April 9. 1940, Norway fell on June 9, 1940.

The main German effort would then be against France. In May 1940, some two and one half million German troops assembled on Germany's western frontier. These troops were part of three army groups (A, B and C), which were further divided into 104 infantry divisions, nine motorized divisions and ten armored divisions. {8-38}. The main thrust of the German Army was given to Army Group A, which was to attack through the Ardennes Forest. Army Group B was to attack through the Netherlands and Belgium. Army Group C was to attack the southern French defenses. Army Groups A and B were to coordinate their efforts. Army Group A was to quickly break through the French defenses, turn right and attack, from the rear, the Allied Forces pressing against Army Group B advancing through Belgium from the north.

The French and British developed defensive Plan D {8-39} This plan anticipated the main German thrust to be through Belgium, as it had done in World War I. Belgium insisted upon absolute neutrality. Therefore, Britain and France could not enter Belgium until Belgium requested assistance. Belgian defense plans were not coordinated with France and Britain. British and French forces facing Belgium could only wait and then react to a German attack. Their military plans had to wait in limbo.

Critical to Plan D was the French Ninth Army. This army was positioned opposite the Ardennes Forest near the south of Belgium. The British and French forces, which were to attack the German forces entering Belgium, were to pivot on the French Ninth Army. The Ninth Army was vital to Plan D.

Just prior to the German invasion a British officer went on an inspection tour of the Ninth Army and wrote, "Seldom have I ever seen anything more slovenly and badly turned out. Men unshaven, horses ungroomed, clothes and saddlery that did not fit, and complete lack of pride in themselves or their units. What shook me most, however, was the look in the men's faces, disgruntled and insubordinate looks, and although ordered to give 'Eyes left' hardly a man bothered to do so."

This was a unit where morale was totally absent. Military power was thus zero. This unit was the first to encounter the main thrust of the German Army. Napoleon concluded that the morale is to the material as three is to one.

The celebrated French writer and pilot, Antoine de Saint-Exupery, concluded in *Flight to Arras*, "An army, if it is to be effective, must be something more than a numerical sum of soldiers." (8-40)}. Karl von Clausewitz, the author of *On War {Von Kriegen}*, compared the physical and morale components of war to the parts of a sword. He wrote, "One might say that the physical seems little more than the wooden hilt, while the morale factors are the precious metal the real weapon, the finely-honed blade." {8-41}.

CHAPTER 9

FRONTIER DEFENSE FORCE

WORLD WAR I General John J. Pershing said, "All a soldier has to know how to do is to shoot and salute." {9-1} These goals seem simple enough. The easy part is to shoot. A soldier must know how to operate his weapon, whether it's a riffle, tank, cannon, an airplane or perform his duties on a warship.

The hard part, for an American, is to salute. The United States does not have a military tradition. Saluting is a simple greeting between soldiers. However, it does signify that the soldier is part of an elite group that has developed a trust among themselves to form an *esprit de corps*. The military spirit distinguishes the unit from a gang of thugs.

Nevertheless, from its earliest time, Americans have had an aversion to the military. In Colonial times, British soldiers were housed in American homes. Since that time, Americans disliked soldiers . . . President Thomas Jefferson said, "The spirit of this country is totally averse to a large military force." {9-2}

The colonies, though, did produce an army that under the command of George Washington was effective enough to gain independence for the United States. After the American Revolution, the Continental Congress said, "Standing armies in time of peace are inconsistent with the principles of Republican government, dangerous to the liberties of a free people, and generally converted into destructive engines for establishing despotism.".{9-3} As of January 1784, the American Army consisted of a regiment of infantry numbering 527 men and a battalion of artillery numbering 138 men. {9-4}

A quality that is distinctive American is individualism, which by its nature is anti- military. President Nixon in his book, *Beyond Peace*, wrote, "Our individuality, long our most distinctive characteristic... " {9-

5} Baseball is known as America's pastime. It is the most individualistic of all team sports. Each baseball team fields nine players, and each player has his own batting average, number of home runs, runs batted in etc. Each pitcher has his own win-loss record, games won in a season etc. The only team record is the won-loss tally. In a sense, all Americans are baseball fans; even though, they may enjoy other sports.

When Americans see soldiers on a parade, they see soldiers wearing the same clothes, marching in step while keeping even ranks equally spaced apart. An American might say, "That is not for me." American individualism simply rebels against a military life.

Another factor working against a formidable American military armed force is multi-culturalism. The United States was not always multi-cultural. At first, the United States was composed of immigrants, but the immigrants came from Europe, which was a singular culture. Of course, there were slaves from Africa, but their culture was not permitted to penetrate the inherited culture from the British Isles. President Adams declared, "North America appears to be destined by Divine Providence to be peopled by one nation, speaking one language, professing one general system of religion and political principles, and accustomed to one general tenor of social usages and customs." {9-6}.

About a century later, President Theodore Roosevelt said in a speech in 1915, "A hyphenated American is not an American at all. This is just as true of the man who puts 'native' before the hyphen as the man who puts German or Irish or English or French before the hyphen. Americanism is a matter of the spirit and of the soul. Our allegiance must be purely to the United States. We must unsparingly condemn any man who holds any other allegiance." {9-7}

Now, it seems that every American is a hyphenated American. President Lincoln had a different expectation. When President Abraham Lincoln first took office in 1861, he knew he had to resolve the problem of secession and possible war. Lincoln was against slavery, but he was willing to do anything else to conciliate the South and save the Union. {9-8} He approved of a constitutional amendment declaring that thereafter the federal government should have no power to abolish or interfere with slavery in any state. Lincoln had devoted his office of president to the preservation of the Union. Unfortunately, leaders in both South and North would not seek harmony or conciliation.

After the Civil War ended, President Lincoln referred to the war as the "testing." For the first time, the United States could think of itself as an indestructible nation. Before the war, The US were referred to as a plural noun: these United States **are** a republic. After the war, general usage was: the United States **is** a republic. President Lincoln also perceived the United States as the nation rather than the Union. In his first address before Congress, he used the word **Union** 20 times. He did not at any time use the word nation. By the end of the war, he spoke more of the nation and rarely the Union. {9-9}

A century after the Civil War ended, 1965, the United States completed a comprehensive overhaul of its immigration policy. Before 1965, US immigration was based upon the "National Origin Law." This law was formulated from the 1890 Census. The National Origins Act placed numerical immigration restrictions on each country's percentage of the US population in 1890. Thus, the US population mix would remain unchanged through immigration. {9-10}

The 1965 amendments to US immigration law eliminated national origins' quotas and replaced them with 20,000 visas per country. Subsequent legislation established a global ceiling of 290,000. {9-11}. America theocratically believes, though actual practice is a different matter, that a society can absorb people from every ethnic group and background. (9-12} The 1990 census revealed that Americans claimed membership in nearly 300 ethnic groups. {9-13}

The American Enterprise Institute contends that the United States will become "the first universal nation in human history." In 1995, the white population in the US was 73.6 percent; in 2030, the white population will be 60.5 percent, and in 2050, the white population will be 52.8 percent. {9-14} At present, 47 million Americans, nearly one in five, speak a language other than English at home. Some 12 million Americans live in homes where no one speaks English. {9-15] Moreover, American culture has shifted somewhat from stressing assimilation to stressing group identity and separatism. The role of the English language as a unifying force is also eroding. {9-16}

This multi- cultural value system in the United States presents a problem for the American armed forces. The problem was great enough when the military had only to deal with American aversion to military service and its individualism. Now the American armed forces must, in addition, recruit from a personnel pool that has difficulty understanding English.

Because of its great responsibilities in the world and its desire to defend free people, the United States must have a strong and credible armed force. If the force is not credible, it is not strong. One source suggested that the US military should recruit an army of immigrants. {9-17} This way of thinking is the worst of all possibilities.

Early in 1863, during the American Civil War, the American Congress found it necessary to pass a military draft law. The most serious objection to the draft was in New York City. Irish laborers refused to be drafted .in what they called a war for Negroes. {9-18} A severe riot ensued and after four days, more than 1,000 people were killed. Army units from Gettysburg were called to quell the riot.

When ancient Rome was in its glory, "It was to the union of the civic virtues and military spirit fostered by their institutions that the Romans were indebted for their grandeur, and when they lost these virtues, and when, no longer regarding the military service as an honor as well as a duty, they relinquished it to mercenary Goths and Gauls, the fall of the empire became inevitable." {9-19} Thus, the lesson from ancient Rome is that the United States cannot seek the easy way out.

Citizenship is a responsibility. Anytime a populace distances itself from its responsibility, it becomes occupants rather than citizens. It has become too easy for individuals to delegate their responsibilities to government, including their security, to a faceless military. A country can ill afford to fight a war divorced of its nation's people. {9-20}

Before World War I, Great Britain depended upon volunteers to fill the ranks of its armed forces. By 1916, Britain realized it did not have the army that would match the German enemy or its French ally. Therefore, military conscription was introduced for the first time in Britain. {9-21} Further, the British people realized that they became the people at war instead of an army at a war. {9-22}.

The population of the United States is about 300 million people. It could easily support 1 percent of the population or three million men for a special reserve force. During World War II, the US population was about half today's population. Yet the US mustered about 15 million men in its armed forces. {9-23} This special reserve force would be over and above the volunteer man power now in the active armed forces.

To obtain the needed man power, the national draft must be reinstated. However, the volunteer armed force will still remain intact. A draft age man will have the choice of volunteering for the active force or the special reserve force. Duty in the special reserve force will be ten years; duty in the active force will be three years. Women will not be subject to the draft. Woman volunteers, though, will be accepted in the special reserve force or active forces.

The active force along with its Reserve and National Guard units will train for unconventional warfare. Some analysts believe the National Guard should be a part of Homeland Security. {9-24} The name, National Guard, would seem to fulfill its mission as a part of Homeland Security. The Reserve force would continue to augment the active force in time of need.

The special reserve force of three million men will be called the Frontier Defense Force. It will be trained to fight conventional battles as was done in Europe during World War II. The two military forces, Frontier Defense Force and the active force, will provide the military protection required in today's uncertain military environment.

During the time of Imperial Rome, some 30 legions of about 150,000 men and supported by 150,000 more auxiliary troops protected an empire of 70 million people. This empire included present day England, Europe west of the Rhine River, Austria, Hungary, Romania, Bulgaria, Yugoslavia, Albania, Greece, Turkey, Syria, Iran, Saudi Arabia, Lebanon, Israel, Egypt, Libya, Tunisia, Algeria and Morocco. The legions were required to defend 4,000 miles of frontier. {9-25} The frontiers were delineated by the rivers the legions defended: the Rhine, the Danube, and the Euphrates.

Similarly, the Frontier Defense Force would protect the United States with a strong and credible military force. The United States does not have a far-flung empire like the Romans. It does have far-flung commitments that it must honor. The Frontier Defense Force will not be used to menace other nations but be used as a force in being for eternal vigilance to prevent a conventional and a nuclear war. If the United States has a credible conventional force, it will not be forced to resort to nuclear war because of a weak conventional defense force.

During the Cold War, the US prevented a nuclear war by its policy of Mutual Assured Destruction or MAD. The MAD policy worked because the US had stockpiled several thousand nuclear weapons plus a credible delivery system. The delivery system was credible because of the triad plan of operation. This plan was redundant and included land-based bombers, sea-launched ballistic missiles and land-based intercontinental ballistic missiles. Any of the three delivery systems was adequate to destroy the Soviet Union. If any one of the three delivery systems was eliminated, then the other two could readily carry-out the mission. Probably the most reliable of the three triad systems was the submarine launched ballistic missile. Submarines moved freely under the oceans and were difficult to track. They also had the capability to launch their missiles while being submerged.

About 500 BC, Master Sun wrote in *The Art of War*, "Ultimate excellence lies not in winning every battle but in defeating the enemy without ever fighting. The highest form of warfare is to attack strategy itself." {9-26} This tenet opposes Secretary of State, Madeleine Albright's statement in 1993, "What's the point of having this superb military that you're always talking about if we can't use it?" {9-27}

Probably, the most advantageous reason for utilizing a reserve force is economy. Today, the cost of 10,000 extra troops in the US Army is $3.6 billion per year. {9-28} One estimate contends that for the same amount of money, the US could have a reserve force five times the present active force. {9-29} Another report attests that the retirement cost of the reserves is a fourth of the active force costs. {9-30}.

Many nations depend upon their reserve forces for much of their defense. Israel's Armed Forces can be fully mobilized in 48 to 72 hours. About 5 percent of Israel's Jewish population is in the armed forces. {9-31} Most are in the reserves.

Switzerland is another country that is heavily dependent on its reserve force. It has a population of about 6.5 million people and a professional armed force of 11,000 men. However, it can mobilize a force of 650,000 men overnight, which is ten percent of its population. {9-31}

Still, another country that is dependent upon its reserve strength is Finland. Finland, which was a part of Russia at one time, has had a long and violent history with Russia. Out of deference to the Soviet Union, Finland made a treaty in Paris in 1947 to limit its armed forces to 41,000 men. The population of Finland is about five million. Yet, it can mobilize a reserve force of one million men, which is about 20 percent of its population. (9-33)

These countries are all much smaller than the United States and are only concerned with self- defense. By contrast, the United States is not only concerned with self- defense but also its foreign commitments. The United States, though, can utilize the experience of the smaller nations. The smaller nations drew from a society that is very much the same. They speak the same language, are of the same ethnicity and felt they were interrelated. Since the countries are small, the inhabitants feel familiarity with all parts of the country. There are no strangers. By comparison, Finland is a larger country than Switzerland and Israel, but the country's population is mostly in the southern part of the nation. This provides easy familiarity much like Switzerland and Israel. (It is noted that the people of Switzerland speak German and French, and the country has a German-speaking region and a French-speaking region. Most of the people are bilingual.)

The United States is a big country that is composed of many regions. There are the New England states, the Midwest, the South, the plain states, the mountain states, the West Coast, Southern California and Texas. Each region has its own language. They all speak English but with a distinct accent. A person from the South may be in Indiana and ask for directions. The person from Indiana will know immediately that he is speaking to someone from the South. There is no anger or animosity, but there is a noticeable difference.

Besides language differences, there is also regional differentiation. People in the far west United States believe all people living in regions east of the Rocky Mountains are Easterners. There are many other regional judgments. It seems to be a human instinct to be loyal to the community where one was born. Manuel de la Crus, a Mexican politician who lived in Chicago, said, "My home may be here, but my heart is in Mexico." {9-34}

A survey of American loyalties concluded that Americans rarely feel an intense loyalty to the state in which they happen to live. They define their identities far more commonly by factors such as race, ethnicity, religion, and political ideology. {9-35} Another survey revealed that ethnic homogeneity raises social capital or trust which in turn is associated with faster growth and higher output per worker. The finding that ethnic heterogeneity lowers trust is confirmed with both US data and cross-country data. {9-36}

Trust is the most vital component in a combat unit. Thus, the Frontier Defense Force must build its formations on **trust.** The simplest way is to recruit men from specific regions with a general ethnic likeness. This position, though, would violate President Truman's decree of integrating the armed forces.

With respect to other convictions, the primary mission of the armed forces, nonetheless, is to win battles and ultimately win wars. The armed forces are not the institution to resolve social issues. The American people must have a single-minded, purposeful conviction of making their armed forces the most skillfully possible. Placing needless baggage on the armed forces is non-productive. The only alternatives in war are victory or defeat. General MacArthur said, "In war, there is no substitute for victory."{9-37}

The United States must be prepared to engage a first rate power that may have a numerically greater force. During World War II, the United States along with the British and the Soviet Union defeated Germany. It should be noted that the Soviet Union faced 157 German divisions; the United States and Britain faced only 60 German divisions. {9-38} Also, the United States almost always held air superiority over the battlefield.

A former US Chairman of the Joint Chiefs of Staff, General David C. Jones (1978-1982) concluded, "Although most history books glorify our military accomplishments, a closer examination reveals a disconcerting pattern: unpreparedness at the start of a war; initial failures; reorganizing while fighting; cranking up our industrial base; and ultimately prevailing by wearing down the enemy by being bigger, not smarter." {9-39}

During World War II, the British Armed Forces were drawn from countries around the world. There were Canadians, Australians, New Zealanders, South Africans, Indians, Gurkhas from Nepal, and many other locations. Except for the Indians and Gurkhas, the British Armed Forces had a near common heritage. Yet, their armed forces were not integrated. Each country had its own command structure composed of its own distinctive personnel.

The Gurkhas, for example, are considered by many to be the best soldiers in Asia. If the Gurkhas were integrated into the British Army, they would become lost or buried in British units. Their distinctive fighting abilities would be unknown. As part of his culture, a Gurkha soldier carries an 18 inch curved knife called a khukuri. His motto is, "Better to die than be a coward."

In 1982, Argentina attempted to take possession of the British held Falkland Islands, which were about 500 miles east of Argentina. At first, the Argentine Army was successful, as only 50 British Marines were on hand to defend the islands. Britain then organized a relief force to retake the Falklands. The relief force was composed of paratroops, commandos and the 7th Gurkha Rifles.

The legendary fighting capabilities of the Gurkhas had preceded them. The Argentine soldiers believed that the khukuri knife was used by the Gurkhas to behead their enemies. The Argentine soldiers sent to defend Port Stanley had abandoned their weapons and fled.

The Gurkhas, whether in a ten-man unit or a hundred man unit, function as a single entity. Each man knows his responsibility and trusts the other members in the unit to know their responsibility. As a result, the unit becomes almost invincible. The Gurkhas developed "unit cohesion" and an esprit de corps which results in elitism. Elitism sounds un-American but it wins battles. Elitism like morale cannot be readily defined but is essential to winning battles. General Pershing's dictum, "Shoot and Salute" is defined.

There are many legends about the Gurkhas, which describe some of their qualities. Generally, legends are untrue but describe a fact or quality that is true. The story about George Washington and the Cherry tree is not true but describes a quality about George Washington. "I cannot tell a lie. I chopped down the cherry tree." George Washington did say, "I hope I shall always possess firmness and virtue enough to maintain that I consider the most enviable of all titles, the character of an 'honest man'."

One unforgettable story about the Gurkhas pertains to their training as paratroopers. To illustrate the story, an instructor explained to a group of Gurkhas some of the fundamentals of departing an airplane. While on the ground, the instructor advised the Gurkhas to watch a demonstration of a group of British paratroopers parachuting from an airplane. After the paratroopers landed safely on the ground, the instructor noticed that the Gurkhas were excitedly discussing the parachute drop among themselves. The instructor assumed the Gurkhas had a fear of jumping from an airplane. The leader of the Gurkhas explained that the men had no fear of jumping from an airplane. They wondered if they might use parachutes the first time.

"The NATO alliance is effective because of its strong cultural and ethnic base". {9-40} This same base concept may also be applied to form military units. Ethnic units may be formed from each geographic region in the United States. Men in these units will immediately bond because of a common culture and their coming from towns familiar to every man. They realize they are neighbors. A trust immediately develops.

The United States is the fourth largest country in the world with the third largest population. Being large and having a large population, it is bound to develop many cultures over time. It has taken two centuries to develop, and it is still developing. New immigrants from Asia and Latin America are changing the culture of America.

According to historian David Hackett Fisher who wrote *Remapping*

American Culture, America originally was composed of four cultures. The English settlers merely brought their culture with them when they came to America. The four cultures were Puritan, Quakers, Cavaliers and Back Country Farmers. With new immigrants and the expansion of the United States westward, seven new cultures evolved. These were Northern Tier, Greater New York, Midland America, Coastal South, Southern Highlands, Great Basin and South California. {9-41}.

In Washington, D.C. there are two monuments depicting American men in combat: The flag raising at Iwo Jima and The Viet Nam Memorial. While fighting raged on the island, six Marines raised the American flag on Mount Suribachi, the highest point on Iwo Jima. Of the six, only three left Iwo Jima alive. The flag raising depicts the American spirit at the time: on to victory. {9-42}

By contrast, the Viet Nam Memorial depicts American gloom. Three American soldiers appear to be defeated. Their spirit was broken. All hope was abandoned. The most telling feature of the monument is the three ethnic groups represented by the three soldiers. One is Hispanic; one is Anglo, and one is Black. This also shows the effects of multi- cultural presumption in the United States.

Claritas, a marketing firm, breaks down the US population into 62 psycho demographic clusters {9-43} The motto of the United States is: e pluribus unum, one out of many. The United States may abide by its motto, but it must realize that the nation is composed of many different groups. Once this fact is accepted, it can be used to its advantage. Men from the same region and ethnic group will bond into a strong fighting unit.

The United States has had experiences with ethnic fighting units. During World War I, an all- black volunteer unit, the US Harlem Hell Fighters, was formed into the 369th Regiment that was attached to the French 16th Division. The Hell Fighters were in combat longer than any other American unit. France awarded the unit 171 *Cruix de Guerre*, an award given to officers and men for gallant action *in war.*

Before World War I, an all black unit called Buffalo Soldiers by the Cheyenne Indians, helped tame the American West. The unit won 23 Congressional Medals of Honor. At one time, it marched 108 miles in a blizzard to relieve some beleaguered soldiers. {9-44}

During World War II, Japanese Americans volunteered to fight for the United States. A total of 30,000 Nisei volunteered. At first, they formed the 100th Infantry Battalion. Later, the unit became the 442

Regimental Combat Team. The unit fought in Italy and received a high proportion of Purple Hearts. {9-45}

These are examples of three American combat units drawn from ethnic groups. There are others. When a military unit is formed with similar ethnicity and combined with same regional backgrounds, a strong bond and trust results. Mostly, this goal can readily be achieved. However, exceptions may be anticipated. Some men will have dual ethnicity, and some may not have strong regional attachments. This problem may be resolved by placing such men in The American Eagle battalion. This unit will also accommodate men who are not comfortable with their ethnicity. A Chinese-American whose parents and grandparents were born in the United States may not feel that he is Chinese. He may not be able to speak Chinese and does not like Chinese food. This man would fit well into the American Eagle battalion.

Homosexuals and women volunteers will find a place in the Frontier Defense Force. Women will be trained as occupation police. When enemy territory is overrun, a police force friendly to the United States must be in place. The American police force will seek cooperation from the indigenous police establishment to bring about law and order.

During the Gulf War, women had proved that they can be excellent combat personnel. They can fly a plane as well as a man; they can shoot a rifle as well as a man, and they can march as well as a man. Unfortunately, they are a detriment to trust, unit cohesion and esprit de corps, which influence morale. Yet, they may still serve their country by being in all-women units. In addition, they may serve in administrative areas.

Homosexuals will be in separate units and trained as commandos. They will seek and destroy guerrilla and partisan bands that operate behind friendly and enemy lines. . According to homosexual activists ten percent of American males are gay. Another source claims that only one percent are gay. {9-46}

Before the men are formed into battalions, they will undergo basic training. All men will be trained as infantrymen. Later, they will receive specialized training. Being a trained infantryman is very consequential, as no one can predict future circumstances.

In 1942, during the Philippine campaign in World War II, the Japanese Army was ordered to overrun and take possession of the Philippine Islands. The American defense was predicated on the interception of the Japanese invading force by the American Asiatic

Fleet. The Japanese attack on Pearl Harbor and the destruction of the capital ships put an end to this defense plan. The American commanders soon realized that American reinforcements would not be sent to the Philippines. Thus, to shorten their defense positions, the Americans moved their forces to the Bataan Peninsula and Corregidor. The "concrete battleship," Corregidor, would prevent a Japanese naval attack on the southern end of Bataan. This defense would force the Japanese to fight the Americans on more equal terms. The greater number of Japanese soldiers could not easily overwhelm the smaller American force.

The Japanese did attempt to make landings on Bataan south of the main battle positions. These assaults were mere probing attacks and not major efforts. In January 1942, the Japanese forced a bridgehead at Longoskawayan Point on the Bataan Peninsula. A naval battalion composed of sailors who had lost their ships were pressed into service as infantrymen and ordered to reduce the Japanese bridgehead. The sailors fought bravely but accomplished little while they took casualties. A battalion of Philippine Scouts, who were trained by the US Army, then relieved the sailors and quickly eliminated the Japanese force. The Americans learned the lesson that was repeated many times during the campaign; "Trained troops can accomplish easily and quickly what untrained men find difficult and therefore costly."{9-47}.

The Frontier Defense Force has a difficult mission to accomplish. The goal of three million trained reserves cannot be achieved overnight. However, it cannot be delayed. A trained and effective Frontier Defense Force, independent of the active force, would be ready for battle in about five years. However, it will not be totally independent of the active force. It will require the active force to provide training and senior leadership.

A new recruit will require six months to one year of basic training. Initially, the Frontier Defense Force will require seasoned noncommissioned officers and company grade officers supplied by the active establishment for organizational stability. When the Frontier Defense Force becomes fully functional, it will provide its own noncommissioned officers and field grade officers. The highest rank in the Frontier Defense Force will be lieutenant colonel. The active force will provide the colonels and generals when going into battle.

About 2.8 million of the three million men reserve forces forming the Frontier Defense Force will be part of the Army. The Air Force and Navy will each receive 100,000 men. These numbers are not exact but display the magnitude of strength in each service. The Air Force and Navy components will work closely with the active force, as they will need to train on Navy ships and Air Force planes. The Army component of the Frontier Defense Force will be more independent of the active army.

One goal of the Frontier Defense Force is to transform a civilian into a soldier. "The process runs from the individual level, to the small groups that must trust one another with their lives, to the combined units that must work in coordination rather than confusedly firing at one another, to the concept of a trained and disciplined army or a police force that is different from a gang of thugs." {9-48} . . .

A problem for the Frontier Defense Force as well as for the active forces is finding well trained and motivated non- commissioned officers. Former Army Chief of Staff, General Edward C. Meyer, concluded, "We can build equipment; we can get ammunition, but it takes time to grow top-quality NCOs who make it possible to train and retrain for new missions." {9-49} After being in place for five years, the Frontier Defense Force should be able to provide its own top quality NCOs. However, it will probably require guidance from the active forces.

Men from the same region and ethnic group will be formed into battalions. After completing basic training, they will train for three continuous weeks every year for the first five years. After five years, they will train for one week every year for the next five years. After ten years, the men will have completed their reserve duty. Although, it is hoped that many of the men will be motivated to stay in active reserve service to train the new members of the Frontier Defense Force. After twenty years of reserve service, the men will be eligible for a pension at age 60.

The Frontier Defense Force will seldom meet on weekends. The only time they will have weekend duty is for physical examinations and administrative projects. However, some senior members will meet with active duty personnel to plan for upcoming training during the three week tours of duty.

A definite part of training will be the playing of soccer. Each duty day, about twelve hours, will include two to three hours of soccer. Soccer will be learned to be played as a team and not a bunch of individuals randomly kicking a ball. Soccer played as a team sport will teach the men the value of team work

Other sports, such as football and basketball are good team sports.

These sports, though, are more spectator sports. Basketball is fine but it requires the players to be tall, more than six feet. Football requires the team members to be big, more than 200 pounds. Soccer, on the other hand, is indifferent to size or weight. Every man is qualified.

CHAPTER 10

ORDER OF BATTLE

IN 1911, THREE years before the outbreak of World War I, French General Ferdinand Foch declared, "Airplanes are interesting toys but of no military value." {10-1} At the time, troops on the ground were more anxious of an airplane falling on them than the ordinance carried by the airplane. Later General Foch became Marshal of France and supreme commander of all Allied Armies on the Western Front.

It is said that generals prepare for the next war based on information learned from the past war. At the outbreak of World War I, the German Army invaded France by way of the Belgian Plain, the ideal invasion route between France and Germany. In World War II, the French and British generals anticipated that Germany would once again invade France through Belgium. Thus, the French and British armies advanced into Belgium at the beginning of the war in the West. They set up defense positions between Antwerp and Namur, Belgium. {10-2}.

The German plan, at the insistence of General Erich von Manstein, anticipated the Allied Plan. Manstein's proposed that Army Group B, containing two armies, invade through the Belgian Plain and draw and hold the British and French Armies in Belgium. Army Group A, containing three armies and the main penetrating force, attack through the Belgian Ardennes, believed the weakest zone in the French defense. {10-3} The Maginot Line was not constructed opposite the Ardennes but was constructed south from the Ardennes to the Swiss Frontier.

After penetrating the French frontier through the Ardennes, Army Group A was to march toward the English Channel and behind the French and British armies in Belgium. Army Group A would be the hammer and Army Group B the anvil that would crush the British and

French armies in Belgium. Manstein's plan was adopted, and the fall of France ensued as planned.

Although Belgium is a small country, it has space for two invading armies. The Belgian Plain is in the north of the country; the Ardennes is in the south near Luxembourg. The Ardennes consists of hills and forests with poor roads. The French General Staff believed the Ardennes was impassable. {10-4}.

In a World War I battle, Germany made a significant error in planning. On 22 April 1915, Germany launched a chlorine gas attack on the British and French troops near Ypres, Belgium. The attack was a complete surprise to the Western Allies, as they had no defense against gas. As a result, a four and one-half mile gap was laid open in the Allied line for the Germans to enter. The German commanders, though, were just as surprised as the Allies. They had not planned for a major effort. {10-5}

Had they planned for a major effort, the Germans could have broken through the Allied positions, gotten behind the Allied armies and attacked them from the rear and flanks. They could have cut the Allies' communications and supply lines and ended the war within a few weeks. The German commanders missed their opportunity. They had little confidence in the new weapon and failed to make effective preparations. As a result, the war continued for another three years and Germany lost the war. . . .

On the other hand, the Germans vis-a-vis Prussians in 1860 produced disciplined, mobile, maneuvering armies that seemed nearly invincible. {10-6} At the time, Prussia was surrounded by larger and very powerful countries: France, Austria and Russia. Out of necessity, the Prussians had to overcome their small size with a disciplined army. They studied, planned and practiced new maneuvers.

Had the Germans planned and practiced a gas attack before its application on the battlefield, they could have obtained victory as did the Prussians in the 19th Century. The Germans could have used tear gas or some other non-lethal gas on their own troops to determine results. Once gas was used on the battlefield, however, its effectiveness was diminished. All troops began wearing protective masks and anti-gas discipline became a main technique for all combat forces on the Western Front.

Italian General Guilio Douhet said, "Victory smiles upon those who anticipate the changes in the character of war, not upon those who wait to adapt themselves after the changes occur." General Douhet defined one of the major missions of the Frontier Defense Force. The new force must not only be disciplined and well-trained but also innovative.

The military has its own unique environment. The Frontier Defense Force will not change this. A military axiom reads: "There are two ways to do anything: the right way and the Army way." This axiom will not be altered by the Frontier Defense Force. A soldier transferred from Georgia or any other place to Texas, for example, will not notice any change. The flag will always be near the headquarters building. The Army way will continue doing it the same way.

Innovation will be applied to the battlefield setting. At the end of each three-week tours of duty, each man will submit a report on how improvements may be made. Such reports may not necessarily be written. One definitive tenet will be simplicity. It will be something like riding a bicycle. The first time a person rides a bicycle he must think about braking pedaling and maintaining balance simultaneously. After a time, he learns to ride the bicycle without thinking. The bicycle becomes an extension of the man. On the other hand, a man would have difficulty if he had to both drive a tank and fly an airplane. In a battlefield environment, a soldier does not have time to think. He must have an immediate reaction that is imbued by training and discipline.

An excellent innovation was conceived by the Germans in World War II. They constructed a high velocity anti-aircraft gun, the 88 millimeters. One innovation was to change the gun's direction of fire. The gun was then pointed in a horizontal direction and converted to an antitank gun. The gun was accurate, fast firing and hard hitting. Its 21-pound shell could destroy a tank over a mile away. {10-7} German General Rommel created still another innovation with the gun. Using the German 88, he laid tank traps for British tanks in North African battles.

In 1941, Britain planned an attack on the Axis forces in North Africa. The plan, code named 'Battleaxe,' was designed to attack the Axis' fortified area: Halfaya-Sollum-Capuzzo. {10-8} The British opened the battle with a tank attack on the enemy's positions at the Halfaya Pass. Earlier, General Rommel ordered a battery of four 88 guns to defend the pass from concealed positions. Later, a squadron of 13 British Matilda tanks advanced into the pass. The tank commander radioed headquarters, "They are tearing my tanks to bits." {10-9} Only one tank survived the trap. The British aptly called the battle, 'Hellfire Pass.'.

The same results occurred when the British attacked Hafid Ridge. The German 88 guns destroyed the British tank force. At the end of the day, the British counted their losses. They had lost more than half their tanks, mainly in the two tank traps.

Another German innovation was the employment of their submarines in World War II. Britain anticipated that the German submarines would attack while submerged, as they did in World War I. The British planned to detect the submerged German submarines with an underwater detecting device. The Germans, though, attacked convoys while on the surface and at night. Thus, the British underwater detecting device became useless. By attacking at night, the convoy escorting vessels were virtually blindfolded. On the surface, the submarines had a greater speed than the British escorting vessels. {10-28}.

When the United States entered World War II, it was an abrupt surprise, and, thus, it was ill prepared. The British Prime Minister Churchill wanted the American effort to be first directed toward Germany. U.S. President Roosevelt concurred. The initial American effort was aerial bombardment of European targets from bases in Britain.

Churchill and Roosevelt realized that their forces were not yet strong enough to attack German defenses occupying the Northern coast of France. Instead, they decided a landing of American forces on Algeria and French Morocco in North Africa. {10- 11} If successful, these forces would then be in a position to trap German forces then retreating west from Egypt. The landing, called Operation Torch, was successful. After securing the landing zone, the American forces assembled and marched east toward positions held by the *Afrika Korps*.

Eventually, the Americans engaged the German forces. The inexperienced Americans parceled-out their air force units to form "air umbrellas" to support its ground forces. American aircraft were so scattered that mobility and flexibility did not exist. On the other hand, German air units were so concentrated that, by comparison, made the American Air Force appear impotent. This was decidedly disturbing, especially since the United States had a greater number of aircraft available.

Another factor facing the Frontier Defense Force is cost-effectiveness. If an infantry unit on patrol confronts strong opposition, should the unit leader request an air strike or artillery support? This question should have been thoroughly investigated long before the patrol left its starting point.

A similar problem occurred early in World War II. Germany invaded Poland on September 1, 1939. Britain and France then declared war on Germany. Anticipating a war with Britain and France, Germany dispatched the "pocket battleship" Graff Spee to the South Atlantic Ocean on 21 August 1939. In September 1939 the German ship then began sinking British and French merchant ships bound for Europe. Before sinking the ships; however, the captain of the German ship, Hans Langsdorff, removed the crews from the merchant ships. Later, the merchant crews were transferred to the German supply ship, Altmark. The last meeting of the Altmark and Spee was in the South Atlantic Ocean in December 1939.

Meanwhile, 20 British and French warships searched the seas looking for the Spee. On December 13, 1939, three British cruisers caught up with the Spee off the mouth of River Plate. The three British cruisers were the Exter with six eight-inch guns, the Ajax and the Achilles each with eight six-inch guns. By contrast, the Spee had six 11 inch guns and eight 5.9 inch guns. The Spee's 11 inch guns could outrange the British guns by 10,000 yards or about five and a half miles. In addition, the Spee could fire a salvo of 4,700 pounds of shells while the three British cruisers combined could fire a total of 3,100 pounds of shells. (10-29)

Captain Langsdorr threw his advantage aside and decided to close with the enemy as a cruiser instead of a battleship. After 80 minutes, all four ships were badly damaged. The Spee took refuge in neutral Montevideo, Uruguay to make emergency repairs. Uruguay would only permit the Spee to stay in Montevideo for 72 hours. The British radioed for reinforcements and waited for the Spee to enter the Atlantic Ocean. The fight was over. Captain Langsdorff ordered the Spee out of the harbor and then scuttled the ship.

The Spee had taken-on fuel and ammunition a few days prior to the battle. There was no reason not to use the big 11 inch guns at a distance that the British could not return fire. Captain Langsdorff simply made a poor choice when he decided to engage his one ship against three ships at close range. His enemy could bring up reinforcements while the German ship had none to call. The Graf Spee was a lone raider. Its greatest advantage was to remain undetected. Once detected, its usefulness diminished.

Other concerns are casualties from "friendly fire." A military historian, Col. Trevor Dupuy, estimates that probably 100,000 US casualties in World War II were the result of Americans firing on Americans. The Korean War was even worse. In Vietnam, friendly fire casualties increased to between 15 and 20 percent. {10-12} During the war in Iraq and Afghanistan, there were several instances of air to ground friendly fire that was attributed to misunderstandings between operators from different services. {10-13}

On the Eastern Front in World War II, German Intercept Service operators frequently heard Russians frantically ask, "What are we to do now?" {10-14} This question foretold the rigid Russian command structure. Lower-ranking commanders were not confident of their decisions. They simply did not want to be the scapegoats when things went amiss.

These are some of the problems and concerns that must be resolved by the Frontier Defense Force. Once a problem is resolved, it must be probed for weaknesses. It must be studied again and discover new innovations. The Frontier Defense Force will continually study new innovations.

A significant consideration will be the study of new tactics brought about by new weapons. The United States is probably the most technically advanced nation in the world. This position cannot be held indefinitely. In 1945, the United States dropped two atomic bombs on Japan. It appeared that the United States had a nuclear monopoly. In 1948, however, the Soviet Union exploded a nuclear device.

Preparing the American military effort is to acknowledge that America's military is highly dependent upon technology. Though, it would be ludicrous if the military did not use technology in its possession. One of the US military weaknesses is perhaps, that in great measure, it is dependent upon satellites in space. It uses satellites for ground positioning systems such as unmanned aerial vehicles, Joint Direct Attack Munitions or "smart bombs," cruise missiles and many other devices. {10-15} If the US military is denied the use of its satellites, it will be forced to fight a future war as it had done in World War II.

In 2007, China successfully removed one of its satellites that was no longer functioning. {10-16} The United States realized that if China can remove one of its satellites, it can also remove one of ours. The Chinese military has admitted that it would be simpler to attack US satellites than US aircraft and tanks. {10-17}

A recent study contended that potential foes may have developed two varieties of anti satellite weapons: directed energy that is powerful lasers, and kinetic energy weapons or missiles that destroy without explosives but with a high speed hit. {10-18} China is reported to be aggressively working on ground-based laser technology for destroying enemy satellites. A small missile could deposit a cloud of sand, ball bearing or other hard objects in the satellite's path. The satellite's own velocity would provide the impact required for disintegration. {10-19}.

Another major problem from space is the Electro Magnetic Pulse or sometimes called: Electromagnetic Pulse Robust Nuclear Earth Penetration. The theory behind this weapon is the detonation of a ten megatons nuclear weapon specifically constructed to generate microwave emissions 200 miles above the United States. The microwave emissions from the bomb would frazzle any unprotected electronics within a 2,000 mile radius. {10-20}

The use of the Electro Magnetic Weapon has one major drawback: political. The weapon requires the use of a nuclear weapon. The world's major nuclear powers realize that the first use of a nuclear device, even only one, invites nuclear retaliation without end

Early in the Battle of Britain during World War II, the German Air Force concentrated on attacking British airfields and supporting installations to gain command of the air. Some of these installations were near London but not in London. On the night of August 24, 1940, ten German bombers lost their way *en route* to targets at Rochester and Thameshaven. {10-21} Since all of England was blacked-out, which caused a complete lack of ground visibility, the German pilots could not fully perceive the ground beneath them. The German aircrews concluded that the expedient alternative was to jettison their bomb loads and return to bases in France.

Inadvertently, the German bombers dumped their bombs on central London. As a result, the British resolved to launch reprisal raids on Berlin. The next night some 80 British bombers bombed Berlin. This raid was followed by several more raids on Berlin. The British reprisal raids infuriated Hitler, and thus, he ordered reprisal raids on London. Then the reprisal raids did not end until the war ended.

Though a major power may not launch an electromagnetic attack on the United States, the United States must still be prepared for such an attack. A rouge nation that cares nothing of the lives of its own people may launch such an attack. To counter this threat, the United States must establish an experimental station on a small uninhabited island to determine the damage that could be done by an electromagnetic atomic device. A smaller bomb at a lower altitude could simulate a large bomb at a higher altitude. Experiments then could be made regarding insulation of wiring, protection of equipment and of personnel. Insulation should not be limited to individual items but also large quantities of equipment. Experimenting, also, should be done with securing equipment and personnel in large underground bunkers.

Another experimental device, which is similar to the electromagnetic bomb, is the Blackout Bomb that emits microwaves but does not use a nuclear device. {10-22} The Blackout Bomb as envisioned by its creators will be mounted on a Phantom Ray unmanned aerial vehicle, UAV, and flown into enemy territory. The UAV will then emit gigawatt microwave pulses. The microwaves induce a current surge in unshielded wires that fries electronic devices. Thus, enemy radars and surveillance stations will be disabled. In a sense, the enemy will be blind. Opposing forces will then be able to advance unhindered.

The United States must confront another technological weakness: cyberattacks. "These attacks can be designed to steal our nation's intellectual property or manipulate information to cause financial, logistical, or military chaos." {10-23}. Recently, Estonia underwent a massive cyberattack that shut down many government networks and forced its largest bank to close its web site.

Therefore, the United States must be prepared to fight a war with technology or without technology. It is possible that the United States may be forced to fight a war with only a partial black out of technology. The Frontier Defense Force must not only be prepared to fight a war with full technological support but also it must also be prepared to fight a war without satellite technology.

In a worst case scenario, the Frontier Defense Force must be prepared to fight a war without any electronic technology. Horses and mules may be the chief vehicles for transportation. Steam technology may make a comeback.

The Frontier Defense Force must be prepared to fight the demands of three kinds of warfare :(1) full technological support, (2) a war without satellite support, and (3) a complete void of electronic technology. Therefore, the Frontier Defense force will train for three wartime possibilities. Each unit will train for one of three types of warfare. If war comes, the United States should be prepared .for three different types of war. It will be the responsibility of the unit trained for the upcoming war to prepare the other two units on what to expect in another type of warfare.

After World War I, France put its faith in the Maginot Line to protect it from a German invasion. The Maginot Line was a series of concrete forts along the German frontier extending from Switzerland to Luxembourg. The forts were placed about three miles apart with smaller casemates placed between the forts. The forts and casemates were underground except for a visible observation dome and gun turret The Maginot Line was built to satisfy the military, political, diplomatic, and financial circumstances. {10-24}. Consequently, when German armored forces pushed through the Ardennes, north of the Maginot limit, and entered France, French forces disintegrated. The French prime minister began talking of defeat. France had developed a "Maginot Mentality." It had put all its trust in the Maginot Line, and when it failed, France felt doomed.

For France, this was *a test* of will. Their Maginot .Line had not performed as anticipated. The enormous casualties of World War I would be duplicated in World War II. Even though, at the time, the French Army was about equal to the German Army. Germany had 136 divisions in the West of which 10 were tank divisions. The French, British and Belgians had 126 divisions. Three were tank divisions. France had 3,254 tanks while Germany had 2,574 tanks. (10-25) The French, however, used most of their tanks to support their infantry units. The Germans, on the other hand, used most of their tanks in separate armored or panzer divisions. The German panzer divisions backed-up by Stuka dive bombers quickly broke through the Allied forces at Sedan and advanced north to the English Channel. The two panzer leaders, Generals Guderian and Rommel, raced to the English Channel. They reached the channel seven days after the initial breakthrough of the French defenses. At this time, France had an excellent opportunity to launch a strong counter-attack. The German Army was strung-out for miles. The infantry and heavy artillery could not keep pace with the armored units. Thus, confusion and disorganization would complicate German defenses.

France still had adequate strength to launch a powerful counterattack. The troops manning the Maginot Line and troops holding positions in eastern France were available for battle. (10-26) The Germans also believed that a French counter-attack .was possible and declined to use its panzer forces to defeat the Allied Forces at Dunkirk. French leaders, though, delayed making a decision. Every passing day of delay diminished the prospects of a successful French counter-attack. Consequently, the Fall of France was inevitable.

The US Frontier Defense Force will not react like the French Army. In a crisis it will seek victory and nothing less. If America is forced into a war, the Frontier Defense Force will shorten the war because of the Force's combat training and discipline. In addition, the Force will reduce casualties. A trained and disciplined Force will inflict heavy casualties on the enemy while enduring only light casualties on itself.

Early in World War II, Japan overran most of the land area in the Western Pacific Ocean in less than a year. It took almost three years to drive the Japanese forces back to Japan. Being unprepared for war, the United States offered Japan an opportunity to risk war. Incidental to the Japanese conquest was the American and allied prisoners taken by Japan. Japan captured 12,000 Americans and 60,000 Filipinos in the Philippine Islands. About two months earlier, the British troops at Singapore surrendered to Japan. There were about 70,000 British and Australian troops at Singapore. (10-27).

A Frontier Defense Force will protect America from a long and costly war. It will not only protect America, but also Western Civilization. A speech by Winston Churchill in 1940 reads in part: "If we can stand up to him all Europe may be freed and the life of the world may move forward into broad sunlit uplands..." America will take on the responsibility of the Greeks at Salamis in 480 B.C. This will be **America's resolve to secure liberty for the free world.**

BIBLIOGRAPHY

Books

American Heritage, *History of World War I*, American Heritage Publishing Company, Ind., NY, NY

Evans, Robert F.*Legions of Imperial Rome*, Vantage Press, New York

Black, Jeremy, *The Seventy Great Battles in History*, Thames & Hudson Ltd., London

Buchanan, Patrick J., *A Republic, Not an Empire*, Regency Publishing Inc., Washington, D.C.

Butler, Rupert, *The Black Angels*, St. Martins Press, NY, NY

Childs, John, *A Dictionary of Military History and Art of War*, The Spartan Press, Cornwall, Great Britain

Churchill, Winston S., *I, The Gathering Storm* and *II, Their Finest Hour*, Houghton Mifflin Company, Boston

Deighton, Len, *Blitzkrieg*, Alfred A. Knopf, N.Y., N.Y.

Doening, David, *The Devil's Virtuosos*, St. Martin's Press, N. Y, NY

Dunnigan, James F.,*How to Make War*, William Morrow & Company. Inc., N. Y., N Y.

Dupuy, Ernest R. and Trevor N. Dupuy, *The Encyclopedia of Military History*, Harper & Row, New York.

Glines, Carrol V., *Doolittle's Tokyo Raiders*, Van Nostrand Reinhold Company, N/Y., N.Y.

Graber, G. S., *The History of the SS*, David McKay Company, Inc., N.Y. N.Y.

Hart, Liddell B. A., *The Rommel Papers*, Harcourt, Brace & Company, N.Y., N.Y

Hammerton, Sir John, Dr. Harry Elmer Barnes and Bruce C. Hopper, *The Illustrated World History*, Wm. H. Wise & Co., New York.

Herman, Arthur, *To Rule the Waves*, Harper Collins Publishers, N.Y., N.Y.

Holmes, Richard, *The Oxford Companion to Military History*, Oxford University Press, N.Y. N.Y.

Hoyt, Edwin P., *America's Wars and Military Excursions*, McGraw-Hill Book Co,, N.Y., N.Y.

Jblonski, Edward, *A Pictorial History of the Middle East* and *A Pictorial History of the World War II Years*, Doubleday & Co., Inc., Garden City, N.Y. N.Y.

Johnson, Curtm *Artillery*, Octopus Books Limited, London

Keegan, John and Richard Holmes, *Soldiers*, Viking Penguin, Inc., N.Y., N.Y.

Keegan, John and Andrew Wheatcroft, *Zones of Conflict*, Simon & Schuster, N.Y. N.Y.

Kerr, Walter, *The Secret of Stalingrad*, Doubleday & Co., Inc. Garden City, N.Y.

Koch, H. W., *A History of Prussia*, Barnes & Noble Books, N.Y.

Langer, William L., *An Encyclopedia of World History*, Harvard University, Houghton Mifflin Company, Boston

Life World Library, *Greece*, and *Germany*. and *Handbook of the Nations* and *Israel*, Time, Inc., N.Y., N.Y.

Luttwak, Edward N., *The Pentagon and the Art of War*, Simon & Schuster, N.Y., N.Y.

Middleton, Drew, *Can America Win the Next War*, Charles Scribner' Sons, N.Y., N.Y.

Morris, Eric, *Corregidor*, Stein & Day, Briarcliff Manor, N.Y.

Newsweek, *The Five Worlds of Our Lives*, C.S. Hammond & Co., N.Y.

Nixon, Richard, *Beyond Peace*, Random House, N.Y.

Petre, F.Loraine, *Napoleon At War*, Hippocrene Books, Inc., New York

Quick, John, *Dictionary of Weapons and Military Tactics*, McGraw Hill Book Co., San Francisco

Regan, Geoffrey, *Decisive Battles*, Canopy Books, NY

Sears, Stephen W., *Desert War in North Africa*, American Heritage Publishing Co., Inc., NY

Sun-tzu, *The Art of War*, Penguin Putnam, Inc. N.Y.

Young, Desmond, *Rommel, The Desert Fox*, Harper Brothers, N.Y...

Periodicals

Air Force Magazine, Air Force Association, Arlington, Va.
The Barnes Review, Washington, D.C.
Current History, Philadelphia, Pa
The Economist Magazine, N.Y.
National Defense Magazine, .National Defense Industrial Association, Arlington, Va.
Newsweek Magazine, Harlan, Ia.
Officer Magazine, Reserve Officers Association of the United States, Washington, D.C.
Imprimis, Hillsdale College, Hillsdale, Michigan
Popular Science Magazine, N.Y.
Time Magazine, N.Y.
U.S. News & World Report Magazine, N.Y.
Wilson Quarterly, One Woodrow Wilson Plaza, 1300 Pennsylvania Ave., NW, Washington, DC

Miscellaneous

Childers, Thomas, Professor of History , University of Pennsylvania, *A History of Hitler's Empire*
Huston, Col. James A., Military Review, Vol. 8-70, pp 83-90, U.S. Army General Staff College, Ft. Leavenworth, Kansas

END NOTES

Note No.

P-1 Life, Handbook of the Nations, 97
P-2 Luttwak, 270
1-1 Newsweek, The Five Worlds of Our Lives, 93
1-2 Churchill-I, 10
1-3 Hammerton, 1145
1-4-ibid 977
1-5-Ibid 977
1-6-ibid-979
1-7-bid-981
1-8-American Heritage, History of World War I 18
1-9-Hammerton-op. cit.981
1-10-ibid 985
1-11-ibid-984
1-12-ibid-984
1-13-ibid-985
1-14-ibid 985
1-15-ibid-986
1-16=American Heritage History of World War I 34
1-17-ibid-41
1-18-ibid 41
1-19-ibid 35
1-20-Dupuy-9171-21=American Heritage History of World War I 20
1-22-ibid 43
1-23=ibid 76
11-24-ibid 77
1-25-Hammerton, op. Cit. 1146
1-26-American Heritage History of World War I 79

1-27-U:.S. News & World Report (April-4-05) 39
1-28-American Heritage History of World War I 77
1-29-ibid 103
1-30-ibid 133
1-31-Dupuy, op. Cit. 948
1-32-Johnson 100
1-33-Dupuy, op, cit. 990
1-34-Hammerton op.cit.-1145
1-35-Holmes, 746
1-36-Hammerton, op.cit. 1147
1-37-Newsweek, The Five Worlds of Our Lives, 166
1-38-Hammerton, op.cit. 1152
1-39-ibid. 1151
1-40-ibid. 1147
1-41-ibid. 1149
1-42-Hoyt 250
1-43-Langer 817
1-44-ibid. 817
145-Hoyt op. cit. 266
1-46-Air Force Magazine April 07-64
147-ibid. 64
1-48-ibid. 64
1-49-Childs-850
1-50-Holmes, op.cit. 954
1-51-Hammerton, op.cit. 1094
1-52-ibid. 1095
1-53-;;ibid. 1095
154-Newsweek, The Five Worlds of Our Lives 130
1-55-Hammerton, op. cit. 1161
1-56-ibid., 1163
1-57-ibid. 1164
1-58-ibid. 1166
1-59-Churchill-I op.cit. 194
1-60-ibid. 193
1-61-ibid. 211
1-62-Hammerton, op.cit. 1174
1-63-;ibid. 1174
1-64--Churchill-I op. Cit. 286
1-65-ibid. 287

1-66-ibid. 310

1-67-ibid. 311

1-68-Hammerton, op.cit. 1177

1-69-Churchill-I op.cit 302

1-70-Hammerton, op. cit. 1177

1-71-Churchill-I op.cit. 312

1-72-ibid. 311

1-73-ibid. 299

1-74-ibid. 309

1-75- ibid. 290

1-76-ibid. 315

1-77-ibid. 317

1-78-ibid. 3-319

1-79-ibid. 318

1-80-ibid. 321

1-81-ibid. 301

1-82-Petre 30

1-83- Churchill I-op. cit. iv

1-84-Holmes-op. cit., 1004

2-1-Life World Library, Germany 35

2-2-ibid. 36

2-3-Koch, 250

2-4-Holmes, op.cit. 113

2-5-Koch, op. cit. 260

2-6-Johnson, op. cit., 28

2-7-Regan 165

2-8-Johnson, op. cit., 28

2-9-Hudson 216

2-10-Regan, op.cit., 165

2-11-ibid. 167

2-12-Hudson, op.ciy., 216

2-13-Regan, op.cit., 168

2-14-Hudson, op.cit., 216

2-15-ibid. 217

2-16-Dupuy, op. cit. 832

2-17-Koch, op.cit., 267

2-18-Regan, op. Cit., 170

2-19-Dupuy, op. Cit. 833

2-20-Regan, op. Cit., 170

2-21-ibid.170
2-22-Holmes, op.cit.317
2-23-Koch, op. ciy., 267
2-24-ibid. 267
2-25-Regan, op.cit., 172
2-26-Johnson, op. cit., 29
2-27-Regan, op. cit., 172
2-28-Johnson, op. cit., 28
2-29-Dupuy, op.cit. 835
2-30-Downing 100
2-31`-ibid. 96
2-32-Kerr 17
2-33-Childers, Lecture
2-34-Downing op. cit.,98
2-35-Kerr, op. cit., 28
2-36-ibid. 32
2-37-Downing, op. cit., 109
2-38-Kerr, op. Cit., 239
2-39-Downing, op. cit., 117
2-40-ibid. 107
2-41-Hudson, op. cit., 258
2-42-Downing, op. cit., 107
2-43-ibid. 110
2-44-ibid. 119
2-45-Kerr, op.cit., 241
2-46-ibid. 240
2-47--Churchill-I, op. cit., 143
2-48-Butler 10
2-49-Hart, 321
2-50--Holmes, op. Cit. 409
2-51-Dupuy op. cit. 1080
2-52-Downing, op. cit., 83
2-53-Wilson Quarterly, Summer 2004, 69
3-1-Sears 13
3-2-ibid. 13
3-3-ibid. 27
3-4-ibid 27
3-5-ibid. 15
3-6-ibid. 14

3-7-ibid. 15

3-8-ibid. 15

3-9-Hart, op. cit., 92

3-10-Sears, op. cit. 17

3-11-Hart, op. cit., 93

3-12-ibid. 91

3-13-ibid 91

3-14 Young 121

3-15-Sears, op. cit., 16

3-16-Luttwak, op. Cit.c 34

3-17-Hart, op. cit., 97

3-18-Holmes, op.,cit. 538

3-19-Dupuy, op.cit. 1240

3-20-ibid. 1241

3-21-ibid. 1242

3-22-Wikiipedia Encyclopedia

3-23-Holmes, oo. cit. 464

3-24-The Officer (January 1988) 11

4-1-Holmes, op.cit.307

4-2-Jomini 129

4-3-Holmes op.cit. 517

4-4-ibid. 628

4-5-Wikipedia Encyclopedia

4-6- ibid.

4-7-Holmes op. Cit. 666

4-8-Newsweek (March 28 2005) 8

4-9-Holmes op.cit. 129

4-10-Jablonski 228

4-11-ibid. 223

4-12-Life World Library, Israel 10

4-13-Jablonski 203

4-14-ibid 209

4-15-ibid. 221

4-16-ibid.231

4-17-ibid. 231

4-18-ibid. 231

4-19-ibid. 235

4-20-Air Force Magazine (Febrary 1996) 3

4-21-U. S, News & World Report (October 10, 1992) 80

4-22-Air Force Magazine (August 8, 2008) 69
4-23-A-Jablonski op. Cit.-239
4-23-B-Air Force Magazine (November 1992) 33
4-24-Wikipedia Encyclopedia
4-25-The World's Great Speeches 546
4-26-Churchill-I op. Cit. 95
4-27-Hoyt op.cit. 414
4-28-Churchill-II, Their Finest Hour 598
4-29-Childs op. cit. 595
4-30-U. S. News & World Report (April 89) 29
4-31-National Defense Magazine (November 1990) 87
4-32-ibid. (April 2008) 43
4-33-ibid. 43
5-1-Time Magazine (February 7, 2005) 8
5-2-AirForce Magazine (June 2002) 34
5-3-Holmes. op.cit. 451
5-4-Air Force Magazine (June 2005) 72
5-5-Imprimis Publication (September 2008)) 4
5-6-ibid. 5
6-1-Life World Library, Greece 28
6-2-Holmes op.cit, 414
6-3-Dupuy op.cit, 25
6-4-ibid 26
6-5-Quick 449
6-6-ibid. 226
6-7-Regan 10
6-8-ibid. 10
6-9-Dupuy op.cit. 23
6-10-Hudson op.cit. 23
6-11-Dupuy op.cit. 27
6-11-ibid. 10
6-12-Life World Library, Greece 30
6-13-Hudson op. cit.26
6-14-Dupuy op.cit 27
6-15-Life World Library, Greece 102
6-16-Nixon 173
6-17-Herman 551
6-18-Copeland 474
6-19-The Economist Magazine (June 29, 2002) 6

6-20-Dupuy op.cit. 780
6-21-U. S. News & World Report (February 25, 2002) 20
6-22-Nixon op.cit. 14
6-23-U. S. News & World Report (January 26, 1987) 21
7-1.Dupuy op.cit. 958
7-2-ibid. 967
7-3-ibid. 975
7-4-ibid. 1090
7-5-Dunnigan 163
7-6-National Defense Magazine (January 2009) 39
7-7-Dunnigan op.cit. 144
7-8-ibid. 143
7-9-ibid. 168
7-10-Middleton 128
7-11-Dupuy. op.cit. 1052
7-12-ibid. 1053
7-13-ibid. 1081
7-14-Jablonski op.cit. 234
7-15-Dupuy op.cit. 1077
7-16-Huston, Military Review
7-17-Time Magazine (Jully 17, 2000) 15
7-18-The Economist Magazine (August 14, 2001) 52
7-19-Time Magazine (August 12, 1974) 80
7-20-National Defense Magazine (January 2003) 26
7-21-National Defense Magazine (October 2002) 34
7-22-Air Force Magazine (July 2003) 26
7-23-Air Force Magazine (October 2008) 38
7-24-ibid. 32
8-1-Army Magazine, vol 16, April 1966 70
8-2-Holmes op.cit. 600
8-3-Graber 25
8-5-Air Force Magazine (August 2004) 2
8-6-Dupuy op.cit. 1016
8-7-Morris 23
8-8-ibid. 199
8-9-ibid. 230
8-10-ibid. 267
8-11-Air Force Magazine (March 2009) 62
8-12-Hoyt op.cit. 418

8-13-Dupuy op.cit. 1133
8-14-Morris op. cit. 339
8-15-Glines 7
8-16-ibid. 17
8-17-ibid. 25
8-18-The Barnes Review (May 2006) 6
8-19-Air Force Magazine (April 2009) 58
8-20-ibid. 59
8-21-Glines op. cit. 332
8-22-ibid. 137
8-23-Hoyt op. cit. 419
8-24-Tuchman 34
8-25-Black 237
8-26-Dupuy op.cit. 960
8-27-ibid. 960
8-28-American Heritage, World War I 190
8-30-Holmes op.cit. 648
8-31-Dupuy op.cit. 968
8-32-Holmes. op.cit. 614
8-33-Keegan & Holmes 39
8-34-Dupuy op.cit. 990
8-35-Deoghton 89
8-36-ibid. 73
8-37-ibid. 73
8-38-Dupuy op.cit. 1057
8-39-Deighton op.cit. 90
8-40-Downing op.cit. 39
8-41-Keegan & Holmes 39
9-1-Officer (September 1990) 16B
9-2-U. S.. News & World Report (January 30-2006) 52
9-3-Hoyt op.cit. 102
9-4-ibid. 103
9-5-Nixon 244
9-6-Buchanan 99
9-7-Theodore Roosevelt 457
9-8-Illustrated op.cit. 904
9-9-U. S. News & World Report (August 15, 1988) 60
9-10-Current History (April 2009) 162
9-11-ibid. 163

9-12-U. S. News & World Report (June 22, 1987) 39

9-13-Newsweek (February 13, 1995) 68

9-14-U. S. News & World Report (March 25, 1996) 16

9-15-Time (October 20, 1963) 21

9-16-U. S. News 7 World Report (December 12,1994) 124

9-17-San Antonio Express-News (March 20, 2005) 3H

9-18-Hammerton op.cit. 916

9-19-Jomini op. cit. 54

9-20-Officer (November 2005) 114

9-21-Holmes op.cit. 152

9-22-ibid. 394

9-23-Dupuy op.cit. 1198

9-24-Air Force Magazine (April 2001) 65

9-25-Evans 7

9-26-Sun-tzu 14

9-27-Air Force Magazine (February 2001) 2

9-28-National Defense (December 2004) 16

9-29-Officer (June 2005) 30

6-30-Officer (May 2005) 23

6-31-Newsweek (June 15, 1987) 10

9-32-National Defense (March 1987) 13

9-33-Officer (July 1989) 27

9-34-Economist Magazine (Jully 5, 2003) 32

9-35-Wilson Quarterly (Winter 2002) 47

9-36-ibid. 94

9-37-U.S.. News & World Report (January 26, 1987) 21

9-38-Newsweek (May 22, 1995) 31

9-39-Luttwak op. cit. 266

9-40-PROCEEDINGS Vol 94, 1968 27

9-41-U.S. News & World Report (December 4, 1989) 60

9-42-Jablonske op. cit. 257

9-43-Atlantic Magazine (September 2003) 30

9-44-National Geographic Magazine (March 1993) 6

9-45-Jablonski op. cit. 130

9-46-Officer (May 1993) 12

9-47-Morris op. cit. 293

9-448-Atlantic Magazine (December 2005) 68

9-49-Air Force Magazine (December 1994) 53

10-1-Air Force Magazine (April 1993) 2

10-2-Childs op. cit. 286
10-3-Holmes op.cit. 313
10-4-Childs op. cit. 286
10-5-American Heritage, World War I 107
10-6-The Five Worlds of Our Lives 22
10-7-Sears op. cit. 37
10-8-Hart op. cit. 179
10-9-ibid. 179
10-10- ibid. 176
10-11-Sears op. cit. 117
10-12-Mewsweek (April 25, 1994) 27
10-13-National Defense Magazine (July 2004) 19
10-14-Downing op. cit, 115
10-15-Air Force Magazine (June 2003) 2
10-16-National Defense Magazine (June 2009) 28
10-17-Air Force Magazine (March 2001) 2
10-18-The Economist Magazine (November 30, 2001) 73
10-19-Current History (September 2003) 263
10-20-U. S. News & World Report (May 9, 1988) 31
10-21-Hart op. cit. 102
10-22-Popular Science Magazine (August 2009) 24
10-23-U. S. News & World Report (November 5, 2007) 39
10-24-Holmes op.cite. 531
10-25-ibid 313
10-26-Childs op. cit. 286